INCANDESCENT ALPHABETS

First published in 2016 by
Karnac Books Ltd
118 Finchley Road, London NW3 5HT

British Library Cataloguing in Publication Data

A C.I.P. for this book is available from the British Library

ISBN 978 1 78220 347 6

Edited, designed and produced by The Studio Publishing Services Ltd
www.publishingservicesuk.co.uk
email: studio@publishingservicesuk.co.uk

www.karnacbooks.com

CONTENTS

ACKNOWLEDGEMENTS AND PERMISSIONS

I would like to thank the Austen-Riggs Center and the Erikson Scholar Program for the writing residency that allowed me to formulate the first five chapters of this book. I am particularly grateful to Jane Tillman, Director of the Erikson Institute, for her warm welcome and support, as well as John Muller, who met with me in the first stages of writing, read my work, and listened keenly. Mark Mulherrin, artist and teacher, was the perfect companion in my early exploration of images made by psychotic patients. I had not worked with images in any book previously. I am grateful to Suzi Naiberg, Kristopher Spring, Sura Levine, and Rachel Beckwith, Arts Librarian at Hampshire College, for their help as I began to navigate image archives and the permissions process.

Readers are gold. I had four: John Muller, who was with me steadily in the early months of writing, Derek Pyle, a former student who read every page of my manuscript carefully and intelligently, Margie Hutter, who read Chapter Two as a sister of a psychotic sibling, and Eve Watson, a Dublin analyst who read Chapter Eight and showed me exactly what was at stake when I floundered with the ending of this book.

There are too many clinicians to thank for work on psychosis that inspired this book, but I do want to single out Willy Apollon, Danielle

Bergeron, and Lucie Cantin at the Freudian School of Quebec for their original, successful work with psychotic young adults, as well as Raul Moncayo and Magdalena Romanowitz, my wonderfully articulate co-facilitators in a year-long Seminar of the Lacanian School of Psycho-analysis focusing on Lacan's *Joyce, the Sinthome* at Hampshire College in 2014–2015. I am deeply grateful to Barri Belnap and Charles Turk for conversations with me about clinical practice with psychotic patients.

Family members are the guardians of any writer's courage with their sustained support; I am grateful to my spouse, Ide B. O'Carroll, for listening to me unfold this project and my puzzles about it throughout my writing, and to Mary M. Rogers, my sister, without whom I would be in no position to write about psychosis. Finally, I am grateful for the careful shepherding of this book by Karnac editors, Rod Tweedy and the production team at The Studio.

Permissions

I am grateful to all those who gave me permission to use images by artists in this book: The Prinzhorn Collection at University Hospital Heidelberg, The Artist Rights Society of New York City, The Rodin Museum in Paris, The Creative Growth Arts Center in San Francisco, California, The Adolf Wölfli Foundation in Bern, Switzerland, Collection de l'Art Brut in Lausanne, Switzerland, The Henry Boxer Gallery, London, and Christian Berst Art Brut. I particularly want to thank John Devlin for his art. His work, and the work of all the artists in this book, underlines how little we truly know of the human experience of psychosis.

Cover illustration: John Devlin, *Untitled no. 162*, 1988. Courtesy of John Devlin and Christian Berst Art Brut.

ABOUT THE AUTHOR

Annie G. Rogers, PhD, is Professor of Psychoanalysis and Clinical Psychology at Hampshire College in Amherst, Massachusetts, and Co-Director of its Psychoanalytic Studies Program. She is Analyst Member and Faculty at the Lacanian School of San Francisco and Associate Member of the Association for Psychoanalysis & Psychotherapy in Ireland. Dr Rogers has a psychoanalytic practice in Amherst, Massachusetts. A recipient of a Fulbright Fellowship at Trinity College, Dublin, Ireland, a Radcliffe Fellowship at Harvard University, a Whiting Fellowship at Hampshire College, and an Erikson Scholar at Austen Riggs, she is the author of *A Shining Affliction* (Penguin Viking, 1995) and *The Unsayable* (Random House, 2006), in addition to numerous scholarly articles, short fiction, and poetry.

For Dr Roy Mendelsohn

Note to readers

I have written this book for anyone interested in psychosis. This includes those who know that experience from the inside, as well as their families and friends. I have written for colleagues, especially psychoanalysts, but also for anyone who wants to accompany another person through psychosis. I write of my own experience, what I know and its limits. It is mostly what I do not know that I trust, the drift of wondering and wandering. I hope you will read with your own questions and the book will call forth more questions, and you will soak yourself through in a rain of sounds and images, leaping from unknown to unknown.

As a writer, I gather and repeat phrases, and each time it is to say something a little different, so that the same phrase in Chapter Two says something other in Chapter Four, and gathers new resonances in Chapter Seven. Summoned by those repeating phrases—I kept them in my pocket all through the writing—they map the territory I have wandered. It is utterly foreign to what I intended. The whole project was impossible from start to finish. This year of writing thrust me into a fast moving river: art images, first person accounts, scientific articles, poetry, novels, psychoanalysis—trying out varied forms of writing and voices (including a play comprising voices) that might carry what

I call "incandescent alphabets"—to readers who do not read along the same lines. Whether dismayed or sparkling with fresh ideas as you read, this book has one arc: to open psychosis as a human experience with language, its gifts born out of terror and enigma.

Annie Rogers

CHAPTER ONE

Encounters with a ghastly, enigmatic Other

I t is a crisp, cool morning in Stockbridge, and with cup of tea on my desk, I enter another time, another space, another realm of experience: psychosis, as it has been lived through first person accounts, books, letters, art, and interviews. Intrigued by the inventive language of psychosis, I think of how alphabets were first made by humans, drawn by hand, and then subjected to new forms through printing practices. I consider the paraphernalia of printers: composing sticks, in which one inserted letters as "sorts". "I am out of sorts" meant that I have run out of letters needed for the line I was compos-ing. And I think of how language changes when one is "out of sorts" in psychosis; it might become difficult to follow one's own thoughts. Of necessity, the psychotic makes new words, and his language carries the sheer inventiveness of his quest to speak, to say what is happen-ing to him.

I am at Austen Riggs, a private psychiatric hospital in the Berkshires, in Western Massachusetts, as the Erikson Scholar. This position affords me time to write, an office at the corner of the psycho-analytic library, an apartment, and a stipend. Austen Riggs is one of the very few hospitals left where psychoanalysis is the primary means of treatment, where patients do not live on locked wards, but wander a beautiful campus with wide lawns, trees, flowers. There is a working greenhouse and a community garden. When a young man (one of the patients) gives me a tour of the buildings, I learn that he and others participate in governance structures here, and everyone has access to psychoanalytic psychotherapy four days a week. The patients choose activities they have proposed, outlined on a whiteboard in a spacious first floor hallway of the main building called "The Inn" in which they live, work, and take their meals. There is a library with comfy reading chairs, run by patients. We walk into the town and find "The Lavender Door", a designated space for the arts that is "interpretation free", as the young man explains. Here, one might learn ceramics, weaving, woodworking, and painting, or engage in theatre productions—all facilitated by professional artists. In short, alongside their personal anguish and struggles, for the patients there is life, a real life to be lived.

In my office, I have collected memoirs written recently and written over a century ago, in the early 1900s. Some of these were composed while the writer was resident in a hospital or asylum, but most were composed later, in retrospect. I also have assembled letters, works of art, texts written into and around intricate drawings, and interview excerpts. Each day I read and immerse myself in wondering about the transformations of language, thought, and experience in psychosis. This is my project: to explore how psychosis changes one's experience of language, what language is, and how it works.

To make this enquiry, I must enter the experiences of others living in another time—imaginatively, compassionately, and with fresh questions. Entering into subjective experiences of living in psychosis (that in our present day have been attributed solely to genetics and biology gone awry), I hope to discover a logic and a language that carries truths we would otherwise not consider as meaningful or worthy of our time.

Who am I to take on such a project? I must say that I am utterly daunted by its scope and its demands. On a round table behind my desk, there is a scattering of books, notes in pencil on legal pads, printed articles, pens, a notebook open for more organised notes, and art materials, for those moments when I am beyond any comprehension, any words to convey what I am discovering. To enter this project fully, I not only have to read and immerse myself in the experiences of others I have never met, I have also to keep company with my own past. As a young person of sixteen, I was a patient in a private psychiatric hospital where I encountered locked wards. I was treated as mentally incompetent, spoken about as if not present, and medicated (Thorazine and Haldol were the anti-psychotics of the time). I had been a charity case, and the generosity of the hospital ran out when my diagnosis was finalised: schizophrenia. Much of my experience that year remains incoherent and, therefore, nearly impossible to narrate, yet unforgettable.

I lived in psychosis for the greater part of two decades of my youth, and then, following four years with a gifted psychoanalyst who worked with psychotic patients, I was free. I took up a life in the world, became a psychologist, and moved to Cambridge, Massachusetts, where I joined research on girls' psychological development, and later became a member of the Harvard faculty. This was a long time ago, and in the intervening decades I saw children and adolescents in a private practice, undertook training as a Lacanian psychoanalyst, wrote books, wrote articles, wrote poems, painted and made prints, kept sketchbooks, and wondered, wondered, wondered—how did I escape, when others have not? I married a fiery, intelligent, lovely Irish woman, and built a life in two places, two nations. I sang, danced, travelled, and experienced that great adventure of loving someone deeply, intimately, and over a long time. I moved to Western Massachusetts twelve years ago, to Hampshire College in Amherst, a unique place where young people are responsible for their own questions and learning, and became a professor of psychoanalysis and clinical psychology, then a Dean of the School of Critical Social Inquiry. Yet, for all of that, as I begin my project on psychosis, I am reminded of how fortunate I am to live this life.

Many people lost in psychosis (for a short time or over a very long time) experience things that cannot be symbolised, spoken, or received by others. I hear their efforts to write and to speak, sometimes eloquently, sometimes in words and forms that seem impenetrable, as both meaningful and compelling. What are their experiences? Is it possible to discern in delusion, knowledge in a new form? Is it possible to translate "incoherence" and discover a new language in the making, made of incandescent alphabets? I use this phrase to refer to elements of language that are creatively adopted when one must find a new way in language with respect to a strange world one has entered and cannot exit.

The heart of this book is an enquiry about language and its trans-formations in psychosis, particularly changes in language that accom-pany the experience as a subjective encounter with voices. Contrary to many clinical psychologists and psychiatrists, I consider language in psychosis not as language deficit, or dysfunction, or a brain-based and driven phenomenon. Rather, the individual's relationship to language is uniquely subjective, meaningful, and connected to experiences that have never been named, and lie outside discourse in the family and society.

For a long time, clinicians have remarked on the strange language of psychosis, particularly schizophrenia, characterising speech as "gibberish" or "word salad". Often clinicians listen to language in psychosis to make a diagnosis of a "thought disorder" or to regulate medication, as though language has lost all subjective meaning. To be sure, a central and well-known characteristic of psychotic language is the use of peculiar words and phrases, sometimes in a context of dis-organised, confused speaking (McGhie & Chapman, 1969). Linguists focus on the structural properties of language. They have discovered very particular qualities of psychotic speech, such as failure to find the right word and substitution of another word, distraction by the sound-sense of words, a breakdown of discourse in associative trains, and the speaker's lack of awareness of strange language use. Yet, many characteristics of speech remain intact, such as the stress pat-terns and pronunciation rules of the original language, as well as syntax, even when phrases and sentences are disconnected (Coving-ton et al., 2005). In other words, there is nothing ungrammatical in psychotic speech.

I begin my work from the premise that language is central to human subjectivity, and that all of us are subjects in relation to our own and others' interpretations of our speech and writing. We seek meaning through language, whether or not we have ever experienced psychosis. The psychotic, I will show, bears enigmatic traces of ques-tions and experiences beyond a shared language, beyond what can be known or spoken in any social link. In psychosis, the subject takes the position of witness to a ghastly Other in social isolation.

As an adolescent boy the poet, Tomas Tranströmer (who would become a Nobel Laureate), had an encounter with "dread" that left him as a witness in language, both memoir and poetry, to this experi-ence. In his memoir, "Memories Look at Me" (1995), he writes,

During the winter I was fifteen I was afflicted by a severe form of anxiety. I was trapped by a searchlight that radiated not light but darkness.
. . . As I lay down to sleep suddenly the atmosphere in the room was
tense with dread. Suddenly my body started shaking, especially my
legs. I was a clockwork toy that had been wound up and now rattled
and jumped helplessly. The cramps were quite beyond the control of
my will. I had never experienced anything like this. (pp. 43–44)

He describes a time of elemental illness in vivid detail:

The world was a vast hospital. I saw before me human beings
deformed in body and in soul. . . . It all happened in silence, yet within
the silence voices were endlessly busy. The wallpaper pattern made
faces. Now and then the silence would be broken by a ticking in the
walls. Produced by what? By whom? By me? . . . I was afraid . . . as in
a film where an innocuous apartment interior changes its character
entirely when ominous music is heard, I now experienced the outer
world quite differently. A few years earlier I had wanted to be an
explorer. Now I had pushed my way into an unknown country where
I had never wanted to be. I had discovered an evil power. Or rather,
the evil power had discovered me. . . . Mother had witnessed the
cramps I suffered that evening in late autumn as my crisis began. But
after that she had to be held outside it all. Everyone had to be
excluded, what was going on was just too terrible to talk about. I was
surrounded by ghosts. I was myself a ghost. . . . No prayers, but
attempts at exorcism by way of music. It was during that period that
I began to hammer at the piano in earnest. (pp. 44–45)

What had happened to this adolescent boy? And how do we
understand his trajectory to becoming a musician, a psychologist, and
a poet, an extraordinary, internationally recognised poet?
Tranströmer, as far as I know, was never hospitalised. Later, I talk
about psychosis as a structure though the work of psychoanalyst
Jacques Lacan, and the way that writing can serve to prevent living a
life in psychosis as an experience that is utterly overwhelming.

What of others, also young, who were diagnosed as "schizophrenic"? I turn now to five writers (Ken Steele, Carol North, Whitney
Robinson, Barbara O'Brien, Edith Weisskopf-Joelson) of first person
accounts of the initial invasion by an alien, enigmatic Other, and the
effects of this initial experience at the beginning of a process that will
be far-reaching in its consequences. I chose these five because in these

books I found compelling and rich stories, and, importantly, none of the authors had a particular theory or angle he or she wanted to uphold as a filter for the narrative.

Ken Steele began quite suddenly to hear voices when he was unusually young, at age fourteen. He became chronically psychotic for several decades. Here, he writes about his early encounters in *The Day the Voices Stopped* (Steele & Berman, 2001).

> Whenever I was near a television set or radio, the voices grew louder and more intense, and there seemed to be more of them. It was as if they were writing and directing the story of my life, telling me what I could and could not do, leaving little room for improvisation. That evening, the voices won out. As my father quizzed me about what we had seen on TV, I did as the voices directed: I put my hands over my ears and turned my back to him. Dad became enraged. "Go to bed without dinner," he ordered me, stalking out of the living room. It was a punishment he rarely imposed. *Ungrateful boy. Now see what you have done*, said my voices. *You have disappointed your father one more time. Your parents deserve a better son than you.* (p. 6)

Ken hears commands in his voices, which he follows, sometimes dangerously. He experiences these voices, intensified and multiplied by other voices and sounds, as imposed on him in a continuous commentary. Despite the fact that they sound utterly coherent and grammatical (and do not need to be deciphered), they introduce a contradiction. After they tell Ken to block out his father, they taunt him for the consequence. They also seem to be able to say/know things that Ken cannot quite imagine or articulate for himself.

> Some time after the voices first visited me, my mother and father told me they were expecting a baby. They had tried for several years, but without success. . . . I did not share their joy. An only child for close to fifteen years, I wasn't eager to welcome a rival for their attention and affections. If I have to have a sibling, I prayed, let it be a sister. But the voices knew better. They had decided it would be a boy, and on several terrifying occasions, they made it seem as if "he" were speaking to me. *I am coming, I'm going to be born*, my soon-to-be brother would whisper from inside my mother's swollen stomach. *You have to leave.* Soon other voices would join in—in a deafening chorus that dictated ways in which I might manage my leave-taking: *Take a radio into the bathtub and electrocute yourself . . . Jump in front of a car on Route*

69 . . . Pour charcoal lighter fluid over your body and set yourself afire . . . Hang yourself in the forest. . . . My brother, Joseph Robert Steele, was born on May 10, 1964. The fact that the voices had correctly determined his sex gave them a lot of credibility. *He's here now,* they said, laughing maniacally, *Joey is the good son . . . he's the one they wanted.* (pp. 6–7)

Ken's fears, transmitted by external voices, are borne out in reality; his parents walked out of his life while he was still a teenager. Ken's voices comment on his experience, yet they come from outside, as alien, invasive, all-knowing presences. He discovers that he can work hard and, to some degree, tune them out, especially at the beginning.

Only two things, reading and writing, could tone the voices down. When I read I entered the world of David Copperfield or Huckleberry Finn; I'd suffer the growing pains of Holden Caulfield or the agonies of Oliver Twist. The voices would then become muffled, like a radio playing in the background. As so I read voraciously. I read everything I could get my hands on, while the voices waited in the wings, ready to surge onto the stage as soon as I turned the last page. . . . Amazingly, I graduated from Junior High with honors. By graduation, however, I had separated myself from most of my friends. (pp. 7–8)

Ken's capacity to study, to tune out the voices to some extent, allows him go to school and carry on, and, yes, be quite successful at academics. But, he is isolated within a short time. His experiences set him apart from both family and peers. The voices comment on his life, predict his fate, and call out to him to leave his family and to end his life. Throughout his account, these voices remain coherent as they command, direct, and comment. Not all his voices were threatening or demeaning; some offered good company to a young man who was quite alone.

Carol North, who would later become a psychiatrist, began having vivid and terrifying visual perceptions and hearing voices as a six-year-old child, but she manages to navigate the world until she reaches college. The voices do not surprise her. They come and go; some have names and they are familiar. The Other that is terrifying and enigmatic is the Other world, a place that can leak into this world. In her book *Welcome, Silence* (2002), she recalls an early hospitalisation as a college student:

A nurse breezed into the dayroom on her way down another hallway. "There goes the nurse," said a voice. A flash of light zoomed across the dayroom, burning out and disappearing into thin air. Had I really seen that? "There goes another comet," said a voice. Okay, I did see it. This could only mean one thing: further leakage of the Other Worlds into this world. The comet had been a sign. "It's alright," Hal reassured me with his sugary voice. "We're here with you." Interference Patterns began to materialize in the air. I stared at their colorful swirls. When the voices spoke, the patterns shifted . . . Frightening. I didn't know if existence in the Other world would be divinely magnificent, beyond human description, like heaven, or whether it would be like the worst imaginable hell. . . . I froze, not wanting to produce further patterns from my bodily movement. I did not want to be responsible for encouraging such change in the world. Live your life as a prayer, I reminded myself. I heard a news announcer on TV parrot my words: "Live your life as a prayer". (pp. 101–102)

Visual patterns and voices work in concert in this passage to point to another realm. Carol believes that Other Worlds can leak into the world she knows. She is not able to control what is happening, but thinks she can stop the process by not moving her body. But suddenly her thoughts are no longer private; they can be broadcast to the world, another kind of leakage. What is this strangeness she is now entering? How will she manage it, endure it, and be changed by it?

Whitney Robinson also experiences something very strange when she is in her first year of college. The voice (singular) came after striking changes in perception. In her book, *Demons in the Age of Light: A Memoir of Psychosis and Recovery* (2011), she writes about her first experience that something is terribly awry.

When I turn off the television at 2 a.m., the house vibrates with silence. Already, I have trouble remembering the resonance of the words in my mind, the sensory flashes combining to form an illusion of meaning. But something's wrong. I feel like a cat in the moments before an electric storm. My mind is a stranger to itself, and its sudden anonymity is malicious, like a photograph that's been scribbled on and the eyes crossed out. I . . . the pronoun rings hollow in my head, the way every other word does when repeated nonsensically. (p. 66)

This experience captures two trends in language: words dissolving into sound and nonsense, and an impression of "meaning". I will return to this duality later as I explain how and why it is that one's very thoughts can suddenly vanish, while at the same time, the smallest detail implodes with meaning. In this short paragraph, we also see a foreshadowing of the erosion of the sense of "I" as viable, alive, and in control, a process that will continue and will have far-reaching consequences.

Here is Whitney again, writing about her first encounter with an alien Other:

> The strangeness is that I'm not alone, here in my bed. I will never be alone again. I feel it slithering out of the darkness for the first time, a presence that's been whispering its sinister enigmas. A living, breathing thing—cold stars and glittering mathematics with the inhale, hot copper and rotten fruit with the exhale. Foreign from everything I have ever known. Other. *Shhh*, it says, though I have made no sound. A rattling snake noise that brings no comfort. What is happening? *Awakening. Awakening from a deep sleep in the dark* ... Who are you? *Lucifer, Legion, Machiavelli, Moriarty, Mephistopheles, I am the serpent, the shadow, the swan.* The voice is almost giddy ... I feel a moment of nausea. *We are* whispers the Other from inside my prefrontal cortex. *I am Eudaimon. We are together.* My body stages a violent rebellion again the ephemeral parasite. Every substance that can be released is released. The surge of epinephrine produces panic so pure it is like white light in my veins, bursting behind my eyes. My muscles freeze and seize and I cease to breathe, and something hot trickles down my leg. *Don't fight it. Surrender.* (pp. 72–73)

Whitney's terror is palpable, and her experience real, as real and indelible as any truly frightening encounter can be for any one of us. The Other she encounters is also enigmatic and alien, both there and "ephemeral". She asks (herself or the Other, it is hard to know), "What is happening?" And the explanation comes *through the voice*, not through her own voluntary, free of the voice thinking process. This is important to note, because she, like so many others who have been through psychosis, will find in time that she cannot distinguish her thoughts from this invasive Other. But I am getting far ahead of myself here. I shall return to this point when I explain how the speech of psychotic persons can and does slide among various pronouns and speaking positions.

Let us look now at a very different first encounter with an alien and enigmatic Other. In her book, *Operators and Things: The Inner Life of a Schizophrenic* (2011), Barbara O'Brien (her chosen pseudonym), writes about the moment she encounters an alien Other as multiple, distinct presences.

> When I awoke they were standing at the foot of my bed looking like soft, fuzzy ghosts. I tried feeling the bedclothes. The sensation of feeling was sharp. I was awake and this was real. The boy was about twelve years old, handsome, and with a pleasant, relaxed smile. The elderly man was impressive: solid, conservative, a reliable man with built-in rules. The third was a real weirdo with hair three inches too long, black, straight and limp, and with a body that was also long and limp. The face didn't belong with the body or the hair; the features were fine and sensitive, the expression, arrogant and unbending. The elderly man suddenly cleared his throat. "It is necessary for the good of all concerned that you get to know Hinton better." He turned and looked at the weirdo. (p. 55)

Barbara presents her experience as having veracity because she can feel her bedclothes, yet she acknowledges that her visitors look like "soft, fuzzy ghosts". At first, they do not seem to be as menacing as the figure that Whitney encountered. They read almost like characters in a novel, well observed and sketched for the reader.

> "I am Burt," said the elder man. He seemed concerned but in a dead, resigned sort of way, a man who had lived long with order and system and who was having difficulty adjusting to the role of master of ceremonies at a holocaust. "And this is Nicky." The boy smiled a wide, sunny smile. Burt explained. I could see why he was chosen as spokesman. What he had to say he said clearly and in a few words. I had been selected for participation in an experiment. He hoped I would be cooperative; lack of cooperation on my part would make matters difficult for them and for myself. There were Operators everywhere in the world although they were rarely seen or heard. My seeing and hearing them was, unfortunately, part of the experiment. I thought: I have come upon a knowledge that is obviously dangerous to have; others would be in equal danger if I revealed it to them. "Yes," said Burt, and he looked pleased. But I had not spoken. I considered this for a moment. (pp. 55–56)

Barbara can distinguish her own thoughts from the others in the room with her. She is offered an explanation, too, for what is happening to her; she has been chosen for an "experiment". She realises she has a dangerous knowledge now, not to be revealed to others. Burt, instantaneously, confirms her idea, even though she did not speak it aloud. Despite this glitch in "reality", the scene is one we can enter imaginatively; we can see it in our mind's eye as it unfolds. Any one of us can imagine ourselves in Barbara's position. And the narrator is a logical interlocutor.

> First things first: "What is the nature of the experiment?" Hinton smiled wryly, "Didn't I tell you," he said to Burt, "that it would say that first?" It? . . . They were reading my mind. I could see it in the ways their eyes focused on my face, the expressions on their faces, as they watched me think. Burt explained: Every thought in the mind of a person like myself was always clear to an Operator who might be tuned in. I considered the situation. Would I, perhaps, be able to think on some sub-cellar level and so reduce this tremendous advantage they had? Nicky grinned broadly and Burt smiled gently. Burt again: No thought of mine on any level could escape them. Operators could penetrate the minds of Things at any level. (p. 56)

Now the reader is aware that there is malice in these alien presences; they can read the mind of the narrator, and there is no escape from them. In fact, they regard her as no more than a Thing, a thing that they, as Operators, can experiment with in ways that go beyond her knowledge and will. Their designs are the heart of the enigma in this Other. And yet, even as we read this last passage, it is not by any means illogical. Logic and enigma sit side by side. This is one thing that becomes increasingly striking about psychosis—its logic is a logic that can enfold many contraries as though there were no contradictions, a seamless logic that becomes systematic, and then irrefutable.

For some people, the invasion by an alien, enigmatic Other does not involve hearing voices (conversely, hearing voices does not always or even necessarily involve psychosis, a point I explain later). In her account, *Father, Have I Kept My Promise?* (1988), Edith Weisskopf-Joelson writes about what she observes of experiences that are strange to her when she is living and working at a Catholic college. The process begins gradually on several fronts, and becomes all encompassing. Her account covers many pages, but here I just give glimpses into her experience as it unfolds by tracing what is happening in language and thought around a single word:

> Things have been so strange, as if books were given me or put where I will see them, or incidents related to me containing a message. . . . I can see a Jewish encyclopedia consisting of many volumes. I feel that the day before it was not there. Have they put it there just for me? To tell me something? The backs of some of the volumes are torn to pieces. Was this done in revenge? Then one volume catches my eye. The spine reads AARON TO DREYFUS, and the next one reads, DREYFUS TO FREUD. From the moment I see the name Dreyfus, I know I have come closer to the secret of St. Mary's and to the strange circumstances which have brought me here. (p. 81)

What is striking here is that objects are arranged as if the objects *themselves* are meant carry a message addressed to the narrator. The enigma is to decipher the message, the secret in the objects, and also discover who directs the message. Edith fled the Nazis as a young Jewish woman, but she does not consider that experience in relation to Dreyfus (the Dreyfus affair in France involved an officer who was falsely charged with selling secrets to Germans. Alfred Dreyfus, a man of Jewish descent, spent eight years in prison before he was exonerated). Rather than considering this case and its injustice in relation to her own former status as a Jew in Germany, Edith conjectures that it is the others with whom she is currently living and working who are actively directing her attention to certain clues:

> Next I remember the teachers in the faculty house. One evening when I came home they were all walking barefoot. They wanted to make me think of feet so that I would think of Dreyfus; they knew that Fuss was the German word for foot. The name Dreyfus means "three feet." I see so many students walking on crutches. Perhaps they mean to tell me, "Dreyfus, three feet" . . . And then there is Sister Mary Elizabeth. I said after a conversation the content of which I have forgotten: "I am afraid I have put my foot in a hornets' nest." And she replied, "It is too bad you only have two feet, because we have so many hornet's nests." Only two feet. Did she not say this to make me think of three feet and Dreyfus? How slow I am in comprehending! But if the teachers and students want to tell me something about Dreyfus, why don't they talk to me directly? Why do they disguise their messages? I do not know. (p. 82)

In this passage, Edith assumes that the associations and connections she makes around the word Dreyfus are not hers, but are imposed on her as a message coming from others around her. She uses a common idiom, "I am afraid I have put my foot in a hornets' nest", but no longer remembers the context of her remark, as she considers Sister Mary Elizabeth's response as another clue about Dreyfus. Edith might be confused about why the messages are disguised, but she does not question that there *are messages* directed to her from all around her. The process leads her more and more deeply into a distinctive logic:

> I am sitting in my pew listening to the Litany of the Saints. The priest says, "Holy Mary." The congregation responds, "Pray for us" . . . The prayer is long. It lulls me into a dreamlike state, but suddenly something strange happens. I sit up in my pew and listen to the voice behind me. The voice does not say, "Pray for us." It says, "Drayfus, which sounds like Pray f' us." Another voice says, "Drayfus." Finally the whole crowd does so: "Drayfus, Drayfus, Drayfus." I realize this is done for my benefit. Some of the sisters to my right and to my left look at me furtively to see if I understand. . . . As time goes on I feel more and more that God sent me to St. Mary's on a mission, and that it is God's will that I should detect something of great importance. The founder of the order, Mother Guerin, is about to be canonized. She is about to become a saint. Perhaps it is my mission to show that she was involved in the Dreyfus case. It is a difficult task. Captain Dreyfus was sentenced in 1894. Mother Guerin died in 1856. The sisters must have forged the date so no one would know her crime. (pp. 83–84)

In this short passage, two things begin to change: the sound of language can slip from one thing to another, can sound like (and become) another message. Edith is not hearing voices, but she is hearing, in voices around her, something Other than what they were saying just moments before. Second, the voices are working to convey something Other to Edith, something outside and beyond herself. Edith now sets herself a task: to uncover something "of great importance". The Other is now a task, or "mission". Although it seems impossible that a nun who died before Dreyfus was tried was actually involved in his case, Edith does not waver in her assessment, "The sisters must have forged the date so that no one would know her crime". Again, we can see contradiction and logic knotted together in a conclusion that seems obvious to the narrator. Ideas that begin as small certainties may, over time, become systems of thought, a kind of knowledge to which others have no access.

But before we enter more deeply into the domain of psychosis as it develops over time, it is useful to ask: how does this experience arise? I do not take the position that psychosis is rooted in solely in genetics, in biology. While there is compelling evidence that schizophrenia occurs in families, families are the crucible of all forms of human subjectivity. There is simply no compelling evidence that schizophrenia has a specific genetic marker.

As I follow the language of psychosis in written accounts, I wonder if it is possible to find traces of the alien Other that invades the mind in childhood experience? Do writers about psychosis refer to any such experiences? It turns out that sometimes they do.

Turning to the accounts of childhood, I am not looking for "causes" or for "reasons" for psychosis. I am interested in precursors in language. I am especially interested in unusual visual, auditory, or bodily experiences that echo with the later accounts. I wonder about any confusion concerning what is self and other, imagined sources of intended harm, as well as encounters with spiritual puzzles or enigmatic epiphanies. Do these writers speak of isolation as children, or confusion about the social world, or the inability to lie (as if others could see through them). These are all questions about existence, about one's place in the social world, and about realms beyond what can be seen, heard and shared with others.

Carol North writes about terrifying experiences in childhood:

> "Pop." Another spark hit the window screen. "There! The fire!" I screamed. Mom pulled me close, so tight I couldn't get away. Dad peered out of the window. "Is that popping noise what's got you upset?" I nodded. Dad looked all blurry through my tears. "Why honey that's just the June bugs hitting against the screen. They're attracted to the light in the house, see?" At first I didn't believe him. In my mind I knew he was right. (pp. 27–28)

This scene opens up a period of night terrors, as Carol confronts insects that hit her bedroom screen. Soon after, she encounters a voice outside the window: "Where's the fire?" She sees a ghost emerge from her open closet. She also finds herself in danger walking to school.

> Out of the sky came a sparrow, dive-bombing toward my head! I ducked, and leaped under the nearest bush. Several other birds had gathered forces to tear me to pieces. I crouched under the bush for

what seemed to me like an eternity, then I jumped to my feet and began running. The birds continued to chase me and zoom past my head . . . (p. 37)

As a child Carol does not distinguish between what she fears and what is actually happening. Birds can form malicious intentions, collectively. We might see this simply as a vivid imagination run wild in a sensitive, anxious child. That could be. But this child is afraid of murderous birds to the extent that, morning after morning, she cannot get to school on time. Around this period, she learns to ride a bike, but as she rides it she quickly gets lost:

I decided to get on one street and stay on it. Eventually I would have to come to someplace familiar. The street ended in nowhere, dumping me onto another street I didn't recognize. . . . One of the voices began to give me advice. "Turn right," it said, in a friendly, soothing tone. It didn't scare me at all. In fact, I appreciated the suggestion. I turned right. I stopped crying, even though nothing looked familiar yet. "Do you want a cigar?" the voice said. . . .. "Seven, eight, keep going straight," the voice said in a singsong way. "Turn a corner, Little Jack Horner." This was getting me mixed up. (p. 49)

Carol finally sees something familiar and realises she is only six blocks from home. But she wonders, "Could the voices have somehow changed the landscape and stuck a neighborhood street under me? I decided it was possible" (p. 49). Is this childhood schizophrenia? Carol continues to attend school, and though her parents are anxious, they are not alarmed. Carol moves through the world; she navigates learning and language. And she continues to have strange experiences. She hears voices from time to time. She speaks to the dead in a cemetery. She thinks her dog can read her thoughts. She is interested in religion, in speaking in tongues, in accessing Other worlds. But she is also invested in keeping an appearance of normalcy. She explains how she does it:

I had devised elaborate schemes to check things out to determine whether or not they were real without seeming obvious to others. I had also learned not to talk back to voices when other people were around. . . . But now with my advancing internal chaos [in adolescence], I would have to strengthen and refine my skills to succeed in the ordinary world. (p. 67)

Carol's investment in finding a way to succeed in the ordinary world allows her to graduate from high school, ninth in a class of 500. Her persistence and dedication to her studies stand her in good stead through college and through medical school, even as she continues to be overwhelmed and hospitalised repeatedly.

Whitney Robinson was home-schooled, but this scarcely explains the extent of her social isolation. She, too, is very bright. As a child she is interested in religion, she has strange experiences, she wonders about death, and she develops a vivid sense that she is different. Like Carol, Whitney works to appear to fit in with peers. She describes a birthday party:

> I smile and eat cake and otherwise try to behave like a normal human being, maybe even one who is happy to see her friends. When everyone has left, I go up to my room and look carefully over my personal effects, particularly the things that are shiny or fragile. I have a feeling that if something were taken, it would be small and useless and of apparent value to me. Nothing is missing, but on everything lingers the ghost of a foreign touch. Something has been here. (p. 45)

There is the sense of an alien Other before she is overwhelmed by it. Whitney not only spends a lot of time alone, she experiences herself as both older and much younger than her peers, especially during adolescence, when she read at the college level and wrote essays on Dante and Emerson, but also went up to the attic to spend hours looking at children's picture books. Throughout childhood and adolescence, she knew that something was terribly wrong, but did not know what it was, and could only refer to strange experiences. Of course, we must wonder how much of childhood is construed in retrospect, highlighted after one has been diagnosed "schizophrenic". Also, how many adolescents feel, at one point of another, isolated from peers, out of synchronisation with the world? Yet, in account after account, I find a sense of childhood isolation, a vivid sense of being different, set apart, and recalling strange experiences—sometimes hearing voices, and sometimes making frightening attributions.

Edith, like Whitney, thinks about how she is different from others, and she assumes that she will always be a child:

> I harbored the notion that I was a child and would remain a child as long as I lived . . . I accepted this notion, so alien to the ways others

understood the nature of human life, a mark of my differentness from others. (p. 24)

She finds it hard as a child and as an adolescent to situate herself in the world, and cannot seem to learn anything that is not in books. She knows others see her as very smart, yet wonders if she is "retarded". The implicit knowledge that children pick up about the wider world escapes her, and common social practices and norms seem foreign to her.

> During my early school years, I observed other notions, feelings and experiences that convinced me, little by little, that I was different than others. For example, although I was considered a bright, even brilliant student, I found myself wondering if I were not mentally retarded. I suffered this painful doubt because, while I found it very easy to remember the readings our teacher specifically assigned us, neverthe-less I found it very hard to keep up with other children in and out of school. The conversations drifted toward facts that I had not been explicitly assigned to remember. As I moved into adolescence, the problem intensified, and I found it even harder to sustain an interest in, and thus to learn about, the outside world—the world of main streets and side streets, the world of newspapers and books not assigned in school. The world of boys flirting with girls, and girls buying cosmetics and standing in front of the mirror applying lipstick as if they were applying their future. The subject wasn't covered in class, so I didn't know about it. . . . As time went on, I came to feel more and more like I was from another planet and knew nothing about life on earth. (pp. 24–26)

Edith is not without social skills. She earns a PhD in psychology, she meets a man who has also fled the Nazis and marries him (although her marriage does not last). She teaches in a university, then (following tuberculosis) in a Catholic college. She seems to be a bright young woman, perhaps a little awkward socially, but no more. Yet, she, too, experiences herself as different and as isolated as a child and adolescent. Like the others who become psychotic, she is interested in religion in an idiosyncratic way, as if seeking personal (not collective) spiritual answers to questions about her existence and purpose. This search happens first in childhood, and again in adulthood as she becomes increasingly suspicious of others.

> When I was nine, ten and eleven, a dream would come back to me night after night. I found myself in the Vienna Woods, and as I walked through a dense forest, I came to a small opening filled with magical objects. . . . The paintings were loosely fastened to the stems of trees. Behind the scene was a little grotto where the Blessed Virgin held the Christ child. I felt the holy aura that surrounded them . . . Each time I awoke I felt sure I must have seen a place like this in the real world. I walked in all directions through the Vienna Woods. I asked passersby if they knew of a nearby grotto where souvenirs were sold. I even asked the forest ranger, and he said there was no grotto. (p. 48)

Edith also recounts going to a Catholic church with a young friend, being called a Jewish brat and expelled. Her family avoided Judaism, and arranged for her to have nose surgery so that she would appear less Jewish. All of these events took place during a time when the Nazis were gaining power in Vienna. This was a collective, real menace. Later, Edith began to piece together the paranoid logic of the Dreyfus case in a convent, and heard the nuns' voices morph from "Pray for us" during the Litany of the Saints to "Dray-fus" (p. 83).

Edith experienced symbolic and real threats to existence as a child and as a young woman. Her father fought in the First World War and became a prisoner. He disappeared and reappeared at the door, disguised as a Jewish beggar. The young Edith did not recognise him, and followed her mother's instruction to keep the chain on the door, not to let him in, not to touch his hands. After his death, Edith feels haunted by this scene. Years later, on a train, when she is leaving Germany fleeing the Nazis, she is unable to lie to the Nazi lieutenants who question her about where she is going. She is fortunate; they tell her she does not look Jewish, they offer money, assistance, none of which she accepts—but she does not think to lie. This is true of others who, as children, feel they have to speak the truth if questioned directly, as though others can see through any lie, no matter the circumstances. I return to this point later, and why it is that lying depends on a particular position in language.

Two of the writers, Ken and Barbara, give no accounts of childhood. But each experiences family as radically uninterested and cut off from them.

So far, I have offered just a brief glimpse into the bare beginnings of psychosis, that is psychosis as an experienced, vivid, very real imposed Other that is ghostly, ghastly, and enigmatic. But the ways this experience is lived for Ken, for Carol, for Barbara, for Whitney, for Edith, and for others, seems impenetrable, once they are immersed in it.

At least in part, this is due to the fact that *what they experience in language* changes who they are, where they locate themselves in time and space, what the body is (and can become), as well as their ideas about everyone who speaks to them (seen and unseen). They wonder if they will ever again have their own thoughts, purposes, and intentions. They have to navigate language on new terms, and it becomes increasingly difficult to speak across a great divide to be intelligible, to be considered, to be believed.

When I use the pronoun "they" here, I do not exclude myself. I, too, encountered a ghastly Other in adolescence and did not find my way through and back from psychosis for a very long time.

At thirteen, I had an experience that has stayed with me all my life. Sitting in a chapel by myself I experienced a sudden change in the light—as if everything were glazed with honey—even as the air darkened. The visage of Christ on the cross changed, too; his eyes, a livid green, leapt from their sockets and seemed to bear down on me. Faces, contorted with pain, surrounded the altar. I felt myself in the presence of something profoundly evil. Just as suddenly, I heard voices singing an exquisite music, although I could not make out the words. After some time, the world returned to me, and I left the chapel. Confronted by an experience that baffled me and yet was addressed to me, I realised that I must be Joan of Arc, returning to do something I could not escape. Two years later, in high school, I heard voices from a book cabinet—and I *wanted to hear* what they were saying to me, throwing my Latin book to the floor to stop the competing recitation, which had morphed with the voices, in the classroom. I began to hear voices at unexpected moments, sometimes catalysed by a mechanical noise such as radiators going on or off. I knew, just as suddenly, that I had been elected by a force beyond me to translate these voices, and I began to work on an alphabet and a new language that might speak across all languages and stem the spread of evil throughout the world. I also experienced burning in my arms, and it was clear to me that the cardinals and archbishops had implanted splinters to burn me alive— to stop me as I worked to translate celestial voices. I spoke of these experiences to no one. In high school at one point I forgot how to move in space without getting lost, and after I attempted to kill myself, ended up spending most of my junior year in a mental ward with schizophrenics. Then, just as suddenly, I had a year's reprieve and did two years of work in one to finish high school with my class. But the reprieve did not last, and I was in and out of hospitals all through college and the start of graduate school—usually twice a year, sometimes for weeks or months—until I was in my early thirties.

Did I experience childhood precursors, as the others have? Yes, I did. My sister Mary, just ten and a half months older, orientated me to the world, introduced me to playmates, and was my companion almost everywhere I went. When I was six, I got lost in my own neighbourhood when she was not with me. Streets and houses I saw every day of my life became entirely unfamiliar. Learning to read was a process of sudden recognition for me; I thought my way of grasping words a magical and unique knowledge, and refused to read aloud in school. I did not learn the names of my classmates in the first years of primary school, and by age ten was baffled by their social groupings. With alarming frequency, I arrived back in my body after being "away", as if stolen from my body by some invisible force. I did not know what happened in the intervening time, but learnt to cover my disappearances. I believed my stuffed animals were real, that they had thoughts and bodily feelings, at age twelve. I was an ordinary child in many respects, not so strange as to attract any notice. Sometimes, my teachers were puzzled, but not very much; I might have seemed a dreamy, introverted child, and that was the end of it. However, by the middle of adolescence it became clear to others that there was something strange about me. I shall take up my story from time to time in this book as I speak about various facets of the experience of psychosis.

I do not stand apart from those who have entered psychosis as an encounter with an enigmatic, terrifying Other. Yet, I have had a full life beyond psychosis as madness, taught as a psychologist for over twenty-five years (alongside a small clinical psychoanalytic practice), and these experiences give me a particular perspective now as I return to explicate, translate, and open up the subjective interior of psychosis, which seems to be both frightening and incomprehensible to those who have not had this unforgettable experience.

It is impossible to grasp how profoundly the Other of language effects every facet of a human being's existence without a careful exegesis of what psychosis is, how it is recognised (and misrecognised), and how baffling it can be to listen to someone in psychosis. I take up these strands in the next chapter.

CHAPTER TWO

Psychosis: what is it, this strangeness?

First visit

D an is an architect, a friend I have known for fifteen years, his dark hair grey at the temples. He is smart, generous, and witty. He knows of my interest in psychosis and has come to visit me to talk about his younger brother, who was recently diagnosed as schizophrenic. He is puzzled by his brother's language and frustrated with his doctors. This is the first of four visits. We sit at the dining room table in Amherst, Massachusetts on a weekend evening in early October. Dan begins, frowning in the way he does when he is baffled.

"What is it, this strangeness? We're losing him and no one seems to know exactly what it is that's wrong, what he's living through, or how to reach him. What is psychosis? How different is it from the way my own mind works?" Dan has always posed questions, so this barrage of questions seems utterly in character.

"What is psychosis?" I repeat. "It's not easy to answer, really." I walk around it, as if it is new and unknown.

"And how do they diagnose it?" Dan adds.

His question sets off a series of questions on my part: "Is it, simply, the outcome of a mental status exam? Or a checklist of criteria listed in the latest version of the *DSM*? Is it, at its very root, a storm of chemicals run wild in the brain? And even if we could map every synapse, every neurotransmitter, both inside and outside psychosis, and make systematic comparisons, what would we know of the experience itself, what *makes* it psychosis? And, just as crucial, what is *not* psychosis?"

Dan stops me. "First, what is a mental status exam? Is that when they ask you the date, who is the President, do you know who you are?"

"That's just minimal questioning about orientation. A mental status exam is actually quite involved when it's done well and includes taking a life history. It requires time and skill. But, for expediency, people do a short version, which is not the same at all."

Dan interrupts, "I would like to understand how in hell they diagnosed him—because he's had three diagnoses in two years." He takes his glasses off and wipes them.

I try to explain: "Making a diagnosis of psychosis is an experience of being at sea among various possibilities: schizophrenia, paranoia, bipolar disorder, brief reactive psychosis, to name some of the choices. Each one is designated through specific markers or signs, including duration, and the way the pattern is distinctive from other possibilities. Over time, the creators of the *DSM, Diagnostic and Statistical Manual of Mental Disorders* (we now have the fifth edition), have changed the criteria for diagnoses."

Dan's eyebrows shoot up at this.

"Yes, the creators re-tweak the signs, the categories and distinctions among them. Diagnostic trends change, so that what we might call schizophrenia at one time, we might not at another. The most recent version made the criteria for a diagnosis of schizophrenia more stringent. The person has to have hallucinations, delusions or disorganised speech that persists for at least a month, and the entire picture of deterioration has to last for six months."

Dan stops me again. "Can we trust his diagnosis to be accurate?" he asks.

"The American Psychological Association claims this version of the diagnosis is more valid and more reliable than any previous versions of the *DSM*. But, to get an alternative picture, you should read Stijn Vanheule's book, *Diagnosis and the DSM* (2014). He offers some pretty compelling evidence that the various versions have used increasingly lax standards for reliability, and so it only appears that professionals can agree more readily on a diagnosis."

Dan laughs. "Well, that helps to explain why David's diagnosis kept changing. He's in and out of the hospital, looks a bit better, then worse, never really returning to himself, if you know what I mean. You can see it."

I look out on the leaves gathered on the deck of our house. "Yes, when someone is in psychosis, it is not so difficult to see," I say.

"Yeah, like the woman talking to herself, picking invisible particles out of the air, wearing an odd mix of scarves and rubber boots in summer—she's not in reality," Dan says.

"Whatever reality is," I add with a touch of irony.

Dan nods.

We move to the sunny front room with hot tea and settle in on soft chairs. It is rare to have open time, time just to be and consider and wander through this conversation.

Dan muses, "But you don't always see what's going on. I didn't know he was falling apart until it was too late. My parents didn't know when I was struggling with drink all through adolescence—not that those are at all equivalent."

He pauses, as if trying to find the right question. "Is it that he hallucinates and the rest of us don't?"

As I consider this, he poses another variation, "I mean, I have had hallucinations, too . . . you know, falling asleep, and also when I've been plastered out of my mind . . . but I don't think I'm psychotic . . ." he laughs.

I laugh, too. "Yes, it's true that many more people that you might realise experience visual illusions, if not outright visual hallucinations, and hear voices. Think of a moment when you 'see' a raccoon scamper over the road at night, just before it morphs into a blowing paper bag. Consider that experience of just shifting from being awake to sleeping or waking up. Some people experience hallucinations between waking and sleeping. These hallucinations can be both vivid and frightening, but they are temporary."

Dan says, "Yeah, I see all sorts of fleeting images going to sleep. And, waking up, I've seen my Grandfather's ghost. I've seen spiders all over the room after drinking. But I don't hear voices. Is that the difference, if you hear voices you're schizophrenic?"

"No, although a lot of people, even professionals, sometimes conflate hearing voices with schizophrenia, but they are not the same at all. We know that about seventy per cent of diagnosed schizophrenics report hearing voices. But (and I hesitate for emphasis), hearing voices is *not* enough to say it's schizophrenia, or even another type of psychosis. Did you know that about fifteen per cent of people with anxiety and mood disorders hear voices? And, under conditions of great danger, people with no previous experience of hallucination may hear voices that direct them quite insistently."

Dan sits forward. "My best friend in college lost his girlfriend in a freak skiing accident, and he used to hear her call his name. It went on for months. I worried about him."

I smile. "It is not so extraordinary to hear someone calling your name, especially after the shock of a loss."

I consider another tack. "Hallucination is just part of being human, I think, which reminds me of a book I read when I was young, a book that really stayed with me: Julian Jaynes, *The Origin of Consciousness in the Breakdown of the Bicameral Mind* (1976)[1990]."

Dan laughs. "I read that book, too."

"When Jaynes used the *Iliad* to show that humans were actually following voices, that we were all following the voices of gods, it was very compelling to me. It really shook up my thinking, made me wonder about how we were evolving and what we don't know about ourselves."

He sips his tea. "But that business about two sides of the mind, hasn't that been discredited by now?" he asks.

"I think some pieces of the theory have been called into question, like the idea that consciousness is controlled by one side of the brain, the left hemisphere—the brain itself is a lot more complex and interconnected than that."

Dan muses, "Yeah, but still it makes you think that hallucinating is part of who we are. Or, maybe it's just that I want to think of my brother as still connected to us all . . ." He trails off.

"I think you are right to think that way, Dan. Robert Schumann transcribed some of his musical hallucinations, and said that he was taking dictation from Franz Schubert. A voice formed the foundation of Rainer Maria Rilke's poetry sequence, *Duino Elegies*."

I can see Dan's shoulders relax a bit, hearing this, knowing that he also loves poetry, loves music.

"Do you know the work of Oliver Sachs?" I ask.

"Isn't he that doctor in that movie—oh, what was it called?"

"*Awakenings*," I say. "Yes, that's based on his early work."

"I remember his curiosity about his patients, and how human he was with them," Dan says. I smile at him because Dan is, simply, so much like Sachs. "Well, he's written a book that documents an incredible array of hallucinations among people who are *not* psychotic."

"Oh?" Dan says.

"Wait a minute; I have it here." I go to my study and retrieve the turquoise blue book aptly named *Hallucinations* (2012). I leaf through. "He writes about all kinds of illnesses, conditions, that lead to hallucination. Did you know that at the onset of a migraine, people may see vivid geometric patterns, very bright, repeating forms that appear on one side of vision?" Dan shakes his head, no.

"And, people who become blind through macular degeneration can see persistent geometric patterns. Those with glaucoma sometimes have intricate, detailed visual hallucinations. People who lose limbs have phantom sensations; in fact, they depend on these sensations as they learn to use artificial limbs."

"Yes, I knew that! I saw something about it on *60 Minutes*," Dan exclaims.

I turn to the back of the book. "And here's your college friend: people in deep grief may see or hear loved ones, or experience a presence in their rooms. And here's you: bugs or animals crawling on the walls are common visions in the aftermath of drinking."

Dan laughs, throwing back his head. Then he is serious, "Yes, but do these people know they are hallucinating?"

"Yes, they know," I say. "They might be confused, even frightened, but they all seem to understand these are hallucinations and don't ascribe them to an alien presence or force."

Dan gets up, stretches, walks around the room, and sits again. "So, what is the difference between these ordinary forms of hearing voices, seeing things, and what happens in psychosis, in schizophrenia?"

"That is the question everyone should ask!" I say. I open Sachs' book to chapter four. "Here, listen to this", and I read at length:

Psychiatry, and society in general, had been subverted by the almost axiomatic belief that "hearing voices" spelled madness and never occurred except in the context of severe mental disturbance. This belief is a fairly recent one, as the careful and humane reservations of early researchers on schizophrenia made clear. But by the 1970s, antipsychotic drugs and tranquilizers had begun to replace other treatments, and careful history taking, looking at the whole life of the patient, had largely been replaced by the use of DSM criteria to make snap diagnoses. Eugene Bleuler, who directed the huge Burghölzli asylum near Zurich from 1898 to 1927, paid close and sympathetic attention to the many hundreds of schizophrenic people under his care. He recognized that the "voices" his patients heard, however outlandish they might seem, were closely associated with their mental states and delusions. (Sachs, 2012 p. 54)

Dan listens intently. "Does he say anything more about that Bleuler fellow?"

"Yeah, here he is quoting Bleuler from *Dementia Praecox or The Group of Schizophrenias*, written in 1911":

The voices not only speak to the patient, but they pass electricity through the body, beat him, paralyze him, take his thoughts away. They are often hypostasized as people, or in other very bizarre ways. For example, a patient claims that a "voice" is perched above each of his ears. One voice is a little larger than the other but both are about the size of a walnut, and they consist of nothing but a large ugly mouth. Threats or curses form the main and most common content of the "voices." Day and night they come from everywhere, from the walls, from above and below, from the cellar and the roof, from heaven and from hell, from near and far . . . When the patient is eating, he hears a voice saying, "Each mouthful is stolen." If he drops something, he hears, "If only your foot had been chopped off." The voices are often very contradictory. At one time they may be against the patient . . . then they may contradict themselves . . . The voice of a daughter tells a patient: "He is going to be burned alive," while his mother's voice says, "He will not be burned." Besides their persecutors the patients often hear the voice of some protector. The voices are often localized in the body . . . . A polyp may be the occasion for localizing the voices in the nose. An intestinal disturbance brings them into connection with the abdomen . . . In cases of sexual complexes, the penis, the urine in the bladder, or the nose utter obscene words . . . A really or imaginarily gravid patient will hear her child or children speaking inside her womb . . . Inanimate objects may speak. The lemonade speaks, the patient's name is heard to be coming from a glass of milk. The furniture speaks to him. (Sachs, 2012, pp. 55–56)

Dan takes the book from my hands, re-reads this passage silently. "Amazing," he says. He looks up. "I've heard about groups who meet to talk about hearing voices. Do you know anything about this?"

"Yes," I tell him. "Hearing voices has been so stigmatised, so associated with schizophrenia, that those who have that experience have begun to join together to say otherwise. There are local and international networks of 'voice-hearers' who protest the blanket assumption of schizophrenia associated with hearing voices."

"Yet some of them may be schizophrenic?" Dan wonders.

"Perhaps that's so, but in the thick of a crisis or caught up in delusion, schizophrenic people tend to be incredibly isolated."

Dan rises, "I should go soon, but I keep thinking—if it is true that David is schizophrenic, then is the only solution for it medication?"

I take his cup, go to get his jacket. "That is a much longer conversation!"

Second visit

I meet Dan in his home in Cambridge, Massachusetts just a few weeks later. He has called to ask me about the most recent medication proposed for his brother. I protest that I am not a psychiatrist, but he wants to talk again anyway. I head out to see him one rainy Saturday.

We sit at his kitchen counter as a black and white tabby cat comes and goes, rubbing against Dan's ankles.

"What is this drug, Clozaril? What is it supposed to do for him?" Dan frowns, leans forward, as if I can explain this to him.

I smile and repeat, "I am not a psychiatrist."

Dan interrupts, "I know that, but we are faced with these pressures, choices, and I still don't understand a tiny sliver of what he's going through, and what will help him. On the other hand, there's my Aunt Nora, who's a nurse, and my mom and dad, who follow what she says. And she says basically—this is a medical disorder, a mental illness that can be treated with medications, and that he'll need to be on them all of his life, unless you want to see him relapse. That's the other side. And what I see is that he's been on three different kinds of drugs—let's see if I can remember—first it was Ris . . ."

"Risperdal?" I ask.

"Yeah, that's it. Then it was Seroquel, and now they want to try Clorazil. What I see is that they all just leave him washed out, not there, and he's gained weight, too. His blood pressure is all over the place. He looks terrible. If they were helping him, great, but I just don't see how it's helping." Dan trails off. "I mean, what are the medications treating?"

I get up and stretch, look out the window. The rain has stopped and sunlight falls through the single silver birch tree in Dan's back yard; the sun makes bright lozenges on the lawn. "Let's walk," I suggest.

We walk over Brattle Street towards Harvard Square in silence, taking in the sun, jostling with the crowds, before turning into the relative haven of Harvard Yard. It has cleared my mind, just to walk. We cut over to Massachusetts Avenue and find a coffee shop.

"You know Dan, there are some medications that, for a time, really do help some people; they help to push the symptoms into the background so that it's possible to talk about what is happening. And medications to help with sleep are really important because psychosis is terrifying, and the person can virtually stop sleeping. The psychiatrists I trust think that it is wise to start with low doses, teach the person and the family about side effects (which can be awful, even with the newer antipsychotics). And they offer something else: a space to talk, a safe space to get through a crisis, and the hope that there is a way through this."

Dan sighs. "He goes from the hospital back to my parents' house and retreats to his room for months on end, and then bang, back into hospital. Isn't there any other way for him to get better than boomeranging into hospitals and taking pills?" Dan asks.

"There are many ways of living through, and beyond schizophrenia. Some young people experience a single severe psychotic episode and go on to live full lives, some people experience multiple crises or episodes that land them in hospitals and carry on with their own pursuits between crises, some find their way through psychotherapy or psychoanalysis, some find their way through the arts. And yes, some find what is crucial, for a time, is a medication that gives them a foothold into thinking about and talking about their lives."

Dan frowns. "Maybe that's so, but it's not helping him. And yet, when he relapses he's gone off his meds each time. I don't know what to think. Will he always be like this? In and out of hospitals, talking crazy, living with my parents, and once they are gone, and they are old now, then what?"

"I can't make light of your question, Dan. Some people who are psychotic give up their meds and adopt alcohol or street drugs; others live half-awake lives, secluded lives. And many, way too many people who are diagnosed psychotic, at least in America, live in prisons, and what kind of treatment for psychosis is that? We don't have asylums any more; now we have jails, and the homeless." I see the look on Dan's face and stop.

"Some of the medications, at least in the short run, are crucial," I say, "but the other side is that many of these medications have terrible side effects that are not only very hard to live with, they can cause lasting damage over time."

Dan wants to know more and I begin to tell him about the journalist, Robert Whitaker, and his review of the "new" antipsychotics in *Anatomy of an Epidemic* (2010).

"Whitaker offers evidence from the scientific community of a strange reversal of conclusions about the biology of schizophrenia. For decades psychiatrists agreed that there was a chemical imbalance that caused psychotic symptoms—the dopamine hypothesis—that could be corrected with antipsychotic medications. Then two Canadian doctors discovered that antipsychotics can actually *induce* a biological vulnerability to schizophrenia, the very opposite to what was intended."

"What?!" Dan says.

"Yes, those two researchers, Guy Chouinard and Barry Jones [cited in Whitaker, 2010 pp. 105–106] investigated the relapse into psychosis when medications were stopped. Antipsychotics cause an increase in dopamine D2 receptors, and at some point the increase becomes abnormal and permanent. Then, when the drug is withdrawn, 'the brain puts down the dopamine accelerator, so to speak' [Whitaker, p. 106], and throws neuronal activity completely out of control, making symptoms worse. It appears then that the use of these medications creates a biological sensitivity to psychosis (they damage normal neural activity). That damage is not the result of any underlying disease, and the medications did not address any underlying chemical imbalance. Taking antipsychotics for a long time evidently creates damage. These researchers called this phenomenon 'supersensitivity psychosis' [p. 105]. The brain compensates by going haywire when the drug is abruptly stopped. That's what increases psychotic symptoms—and that increase in symptoms is what convinces people they should stay on their medications."

"But aren't the drugs supposed to be treating something?" Dan asks, both horrified and incredulous. "What other choice do we have?"

I sigh. "Joanna Moncrieff is a psychiatrist, and she's not averse to using medications with psychosis, but she admits psychiatry assumes an underlying disease that's treated by these medications when there is *no evidence* of any underlying disease. Read her book, *The Bitterest Pills: The Troubling Story of Antipsychotic Drugs*" [2013]. I can see that Dan is distraught. He takes out a notepad and jots down the book names, the authors.

"So, OK, what are these horrible side effects? Couldn't the brain recover over time? Couldn't you get off the meds?" Dan asks.

"These are not side effects, Dan; they are long-term consequences. And yes, sometimes the dosage can be slowly, infinitesimally slowly, and oh so carefully, reduced—and, in the long term, the symptoms do not come back or worsen. But, and I can't say this strongly enough, to just stop the medication abruptly is very dangerous, because the brain will react, creating a state of 'supersensitivity' and a sudden worsening of symptoms. People then might do dangerous things, even kill themselves. So, to get off medications, you really need a safety net and a way to gradually reduce, knowing there will be a period of pure hell ahead for some time."

Dan nods. "But, some people get better this way?"

"Yes, I can't explain it very well. Some people get better, much better sometimes, without the medications,"

Dan nods. But I want him to know my bias, based on my experience. "Let's walk again, Dan. This is tough going."

As we walk, I tell him about my own experience, at nineteen.

"A psychiatrist sat me down, explained that I had a brain disease, and that I would need to be on Haldol all my life. He explained the biochemistry of schizophrenia to me (most of which I didn't follow), and ended by saying that I should not have children—they would be likely to inherit my condition. I did not believe him about the medication, because each time I came out of the hospital I got off the drug. The side effects were unbearable spasms, and pacing. I was able to navigate the world better on my own, going to college, studying through the intensity of my symptoms. And yes, it's also true that there was a real risk of suicide in my case, and that I had relapses and multiple hospitalisations between ages sixteen and twenty-nine."

"You didn't have children," Dan says, quietly.

"Yes, I believed that part," I admit.

"Maybe in making a full recovery without meds, you were exceptional?"

I smile. "I used to think so, but it's not true. Martin Harrow and Thomas Jobe [2013], two American psychiatrists, studied and followed schizophrenia patients for twenty years. Some stayed on antipsychotics, and others did not. Their research demonstrated better outcomes for the people diagnosed as schizophrenic who were on medications for only a short time and got off. And even those who got off the antipsychotics after a long time had better outcomes. This wasn't by a small margin; over time, these people fared much better in terms of outcomes. What they found is that in the first six to ten months, people were more likely to have a relapse, but this was not the case over the longer term. The researchers themselves connected the relapses with biological conditions generated by the previous continuous use of antipsychotics."

"That's the conclusion of the Canadian docs, too," Dan says.

"Yes. And, if the patients remained off the drugs, between four and five years later they were much better off than those who stayed on their medications. They had a fuller recovery and were working again, holding down jobs. This was not only the case for 'good prognosis' patients who had a single critical episode, but also for patients who were had a 'poor prognosis' and had been on antipsychotics for years. Dan, you have to read this stuff. It's in a reputable journal, *Schizophrenia Bulletin*, and it converges with other studies by other researchers and by the World Health Organization. And get your Aunt Nora to read these things, too."

We walk in silence for a time. I tell myself that I should cover all angles.

"The other side of all this promising research", I begin, "is that without medication, the risk of suicide is very real. For some people, the medication provides a foothold to a life that's been lost. Ken Steele writes about his experience of finally finding peace from endless voices in *The Day the Voices Stopped* [2001]. For him, Risperdol gave him a new chance, after decades of torment. Richard McLean, in

Recovered, Not Cured [2003], writes and illustrates his journey though schizophrenia. His experience with antipsychotics was terrible; they were ineffective and had intolerable side effects. Then he found Zyprexa and it was both helpful and bearable. But he does not consider himself recovered. Bethany Yeiser, in *Mind Estranged* [2014], writes about years of living with schizophrenia, dirty and homeless. Her way back to college, sanity, and playing the violin came when she could tolerate a low dose of Clozaril. So, you see, Dan—there are many sides to this question of medication."

"It's Clozaril they want to try next . . ." He is quiet as we make our way back to his house.

As I leave him, he says simply, "I wish we had real choices for him, something beyond medication, but I don't even know what that would be. I can't understand what he says when he speaks most of the time. I still have no idea what he's going through."

He looks at me, knowing my interest in psychoanalysis, and says, "What about that Lacan fellow you have been studying; does he have anything to say about psychosis?"

I laugh. "My French psychoanalyst, Jacques Lacan, relies on the speech of the patient to determine a diagnosis—as a structure in language. He has nothing to say about disease."

Dan raises his eyebrows.

"Lacan is not easy", I warn him, "and it will take time to explain some of his ideas."

At his house we plan another visit, this time back in Amherst again.

Third visit

How will I enter into Lacan's seminar on psychosis? I potter about in the kitchen and decide to make blueberry muffins for Dan's visit. I decide to begin with a historic account read by both Freud and Lacan, and then introduce some details of Lacan's thinking. Yet, I wonder if the Schreber case will frighten Dan, or if this historic case will help him to understand something of his brother's experience.

Dan arrives mid-afternoon, carrying a basket of goodies, a gift to me for my time. I make tea for us, and take the muffins from the oven. We sit, again, at the dining room table.

"Dan, if you have the patience and the time, I thought I'd tell you about a memoir Lacan studied in detail, written by Daniel Paul Schreber. Do you know this case?"

Dan shakes his head, no. "But I have patience; David has taught me patience."

"Lacan says that we should become secretaries of the insane, learn to listen both carefully and accurately." I put the book on the table: Schreber's own account: *Memoirs of My Nervous Illness* (2000[1903]).

"Schreber—where to begin? In 1893, Daniel Paul Schreber was at the top of his legal career, having just been promoted to presiding judge at the Dresden Higher Regional Court, when he suffered a mental breakdown, became psychotic, and went to a mental institution. At the Sonnenstein Asylum he composed his only book, *Memoirs of My Nervous Illness* (2001[1903]. The book survived because Freud took an interest in it, and later Lacan also read it and used it to define what psychosis is, and how it works."

"Was this Schreber young when he fell ill?" Dan wonders.

"No, actually Schreber's first psychotic episode began in the summer of 1893 when he was in his middle age. He had the thought that it must be pleasant to be a woman during intercourse—and he also thought that this idea was imposed on him. By the autumn he had a dramatic explosion of symptoms, including great agitation, insomnia, and hearing voices. Gradually, he built a delusion about hostile human and divine influences, which he described as 'soul murder.' He also developed elaborate ideas about becoming part of the nerves and rays of God, and created a 'fundamental language'—part of an original cosmology. He was an intelligent man, a judge. Once he settled into his delusions, he could go to dinners, and partake in social conversations. In his book he made the case for his release and he was released!"

Dan looks puzzled. "So, in a way he was sane again?"

"No, Schreber remained in psychosis."

I open the book, dog-eared from my reading, to a random passage. "Here, just listen to him."

During my first months here the miracles on my eyes were performed by "little men" very similar to those I mentioned when describing the miracle directed against my spinal cord. These "little men" were one of the most remarkable and even to me most mysterious phenomena;

but I have no doubt whatsoever in the objective reality of these happenings, as I saw these "little men" innumerable times with my mind's eye and heard their voices . . . Only a few millimeters in size, they made mischief on all parts of my body both inside and on the surface. Those occupied with the opening and closing of the eyes stood above the eyes in the eyebrows and they pulled the eyelids up or down as they pleased with fine filaments like cobwebs. (p. 149)

"He's kind of eloquent, poor fellow," Dan says.

"You know, it actually helps that you see this, because Schreber is a witness (and archivist with his attention to detail) of an Other realm of experience altogether. Lacan did not think in psychiatric terms, though he was a psychiatrist. He thought about diagnosis as a psycho-analyst and introduced a structural model of psychosis."

"What does that mean, a structural model?"

"That would take a lot of time, that little question!" I exclaim. "In a recent book about psychosis, Stijn Vanheule (2011) explains Lacan's structural position very clearly. In Lacan's theory ". . . hallucinations are not thought of as perceptions without objects, but as perceptions that subvert the subject" (p. 3).

Dan frowns, "I don't get it."

"Hallucinations are made out of effects on the subject. Whatever meaning arrives, it comes at the cost of the subject, from a perverse and baffling Other."

Dan frowns again, but I keep going.

"Lacan calls this elementary interpretation. He does not mean that it is simple! He's referring to the interpretation of elementary phenom-ena in psychosis: on the one hand, there is meaning everywhere, and it asserts itself *as meaning* (even when the speaker doesn't understand it); and that meaning is repetitive, so much so that it devolves into a refrain, empty of meaning."

"How confusing," Dan says, "How can something be full of mean-ing and empty of meaning at the same time?"

"It is a paradox all right!" I pause, thinking about how to navigate and explain something quite strange and profound. I decide to begin with a form of speaking Dan can recognise. "When I am speaking to you right now, I am forming phrases that connect to other words and phrases. You listen and anticipate the direction I am taking, and 'get' what I have said only when I come to the end of my sentence. And then, you might have questions. Or I might want to go back and revise, undo, elaborate, almost anything I've just said. Meaning is directed towards an end, yet open and unfolding. And, in the end, we can't say everything, just approximations that work well enough."

Dan smiles, nods. "Most of the time," he says.

"But in psychosis, it is different. The person tries to speak about her position and runs into something she can't formulate at all. There is suddenly nothing there, no thought where she (and you) were expecting a meaning. What comes instead is an experience of profound enigma and tension, and then, from outside (she hears it or feels it as foreign to her), comes a word or phrase, or phrases that make no sense. While the words might make no sense, she hears *in them* an ineffable understanding *of her position*."

"Yes", Dan says slowly, "Yes, I think I see what you are saying. Go on."

"The person who is in psychosis builds a delusion, creating a logic from these moments that are both epiphanies and empty, these moments of charged, significant nonsense. Far from believing that hallucinations are just like other perceptions, Schreber knows that what he experiences has a particular status that is neither real nor not real."

I open the book. "He says, 'I saw these "little men" innumerable times with my mind's eye . . .' (p. 149). In the manuscript, little men always appear in quotes, as though he knows they have a particular status that's distinctive from other beings. He also writes of his guards and nurses, who move about freely, while Schreber's every physical movement is controlled by 'little men' who torment him. And he writes about 'fleeting improvised men' that also have a status that is both ghostly and real, creating real effects."

"Are you saying that Schreber *knows* that he's hallucinating?" Dan asks.

"Well, yes, and no. He knows his experience has a paradoxical structure: it is both there, overwhelming him, and it's not ordinary 'reality.' And no, he doesn't know what psychosis is, not as Lacan defined it, that is, as the incapacity to signify his own experience as a subject in relation to questions of his existence as a human being."

"Hold on!" Dan exclaims. "What does that mean, not to be able to signify, in relation to questions of existence?"

"There is so much I might say, Dan, but here's the heart of Lacan's thinking. In relation to unconscious questions about his existence, his very place in the world, the psychotic falters—as if he has no name, no place, in the cultural, symbolic world. That position is foreclosed, and it creates a hole, a crater, in language. What happens is that hallucinated experience comes in at the very point where language fails."

"I don't get this, Annie. My brother uses language, odd language, but he talks. And Schreber sounds weird, but he's pretty eloquent! No, I think it is that they hear voices."

"Remember that many people hear voices, but they are not psychotic. Their speech is directed and their sentences complete. In psychosis, one might *not* hear voices. But something will appear as enigmatic, as strange and disturbing, imposed at the place where there is nothing, where she can say nothing *about her private, subjective experience*. Even her own thoughts can be utterly foreign."

Dan shakes his head. "It's hard for me to understand this. Tell me more about Schreber. He *did* get better, right?"

"Again, no and yes. The development of a delusion actually helped him get better, but it also sealed him into psychosis. The beings he describes as 'little men' multiply. There are many, many souls that invade his body and become corpses. And millions of 'rays' or 'nerve rays' of God invade his body and change it. Though he retains some aspects of being masculine, he becomes a woman who can have intercourse with God, and in this way, produce a new humanity. He submits to his position and his acceptance helps him to be less tormented."

Dan looks at me, incredulous. "Where does he get these ideas? Wouldn't he know how impossible it all is?"

"No, strangely enough, he doesn't doubt what he has to become and that he has to beget a new humanity. Lacan explains, 'Generally speaking, the raw material is his own body . . . in the field of the Imaginary' [Lacan, 1997(1981), p. 11]. The Imaginary isn't daydreaming. It is a register of human experience in which one makes identifications with images to comprise one's own identity. The ego, the self, Freud's *das Ich*, is made up of these images."

"We all create a self this way?" Dan asks.

"Yes. Lacan wrote about 'the mirror' stage as such a passage we all go through. At first, that image is not virtual, but double, and real. And what's more, as young children we don't distinguish our *own* bodily experience very readily. A child of eighteen months might see another child fall, and cry out as if she's the one who tumbled down.

The body itself, its inner workings, how it works, maps on to images that come from all kinds of sources outside and around the child. For Lacan, the child makes a link between those images and what she is, her ego. Before the mirror stage, we experience our bodies as fragments, and only with the image in the mirror do we conceive of the body as one, and then identify to that image. But we all carry unconscious traces of the body in fragments, and the body as Imaginary. We forget these early experiences, but the person who is psychotic has direct access to the Imaginary body."

"Wouldn't Schreber remember that once he had a man's body, and it wasn't all these other things that he identifies with?" Dan asks.

"You truly ask such great questions, Dan. Yes, originally Schreber remembered and he was quite disturbed. He was, after all, a man, a husband, and a judge. But, that was all before he was in psychosis, before his psychosis was triggered. In psychosis, Lacan says, 'The subject is only a second copy of his own identity' [Lacan, 1997(1981), p. 97]. It is the same copy, over and over again. Schreber's identity kept multiplying (and disintegrating) in relation to an Imaginary Other that imposed images, voices, bodily experiences outside his control."

"Wait. What is this Imaginary Other?"

"Well, for example, Schreber is certain that he is at the mercy of forces, beings, that are both external and inside his body. He says of the little men: 'Only a few millimeters in size, they made mischief on all parts of my body both inside and on the surface' [p. 149]. It is also clear that they are in control of his body. That's his Imaginary Other. He tells us how the little men stood in his eyebrows, and 'Pulled the eyelids up or down *as they pleased*' [p. 149]."

"How really extraordinary," Dan says.

"What about it?" I ask.

"He keeps track of all of these details. He can tell us all of this."

"Yes. I think that writing gave Schreber a space to think about why these invasions are happening to him, and to speak about that. The great enigma is not so much *what* he's being subjected to as it is about the question—towards *what end*? His question draws him into a network of ideas about his position. The ideas themselves are imposed (as epiphanies) and he begins to formulate them, through the voices, as significant for him. He has to use new language (given to him) to do this, because conventional language won't carry his experience. This is not easy to explain to us, but he tries."

"He sounds pretty coherent, if strange, almost religious?"

"Yes, strange and religious, and mostly coherent, too. He is in contact with spirits of departed human beings, and he is also in contact with divine nerves that speak to him and are mechanically attached to his body. He refers to the forecourts of heaven as God's realms, which consist of Ormuzd and Ariman—the former concerned with unmanning Schreber and the latter with reversing this miracle when necessary. He begins to formulate what he calls a fundamental language, or Grundsprache, God's language. This language comes from noises, voices, and God. Schreber writes, 'All the noises I hear . . . seem to speak the words which are talked into my head by the voices and also those words in which I formulate my own thoughts' [p. 236]."

"That interests me, what he thinks about God. David, too, talks a lot about God."

"Schreber creates neologisms and experiences time in new ways, and God is in control of all of this, including every aspect of Schreber's position and purpose. Schreber understands very well that he and God are intertwined. It is God who creates disorder when Schreber can't finish a sentence, when he is beset with nonsensical questions, and also when God leaves Schreber without thoughts of any kind, without voices or language."

"Wouldn't that be a relief to him, a pause in the voices?"

"Actually, no. It is most dreadful for Schreber to be alone, without thoughts or voices. Then he is in agony. But when Schreber takes up a new position in relation to God as a woman, the creation of a new humanity becomes Schreber's task, his mission."

Dan says, "You make it sound like that's a good thing!"

I hesitate, wary of idealising psychosis. "This mission, it gives Schreber a place, a purpose, a cause. It organises his terrifying fragmentation and stops the endless enigma about what is imposed on him. He is left in the position of one who knows things others don't know. Lacan [1997(1981)] says, 'There is literally a fragmentation of identity, and the subject is undoubtedly shocked by the attack, but this is how it is' [p. 97]. He quotes Schreber: 'I can only bear witness', Schreber says, 'to things that have been revealed to me' [p. 97]. Lacan acknowledges that Schreber knows far more about psychosis than his doctors know."

Dan grins, "Lacan admires him, in a way."

I smile.

He pauses. "I wish David's doctors had this perspective. But then, none of us listens, really listens to David any more." He looks at me.

"Well," I say, "one way to listen to him would be to think of him as bearing witness to something that you are entirely ignorant about."

"How!?" Dan shouts, eyebrows up.

"That is a fair question," I say, and we laugh.

I suggest that Dan write down some pieces of David's speech after he sees him next—but only what Dan can remember accurately.

"We can look at what he says together then, and see what we can make of it," I offer.

Dan is both grateful and sceptical.

I send him off with my copy of Schreber's memoir and some blueberry muffins.

I wonder if all this talk of Schreber and Lacan will help him to find a way with his brother, or if I have just muddied the waters.

Fourth visit

We are back in Dan's house on a day when it has begun to snow, the first light snow of winter. Dan greets me waving a piece of paper. He has written down a few things his brother said at their last visit. As soon as I have my coat off and tea in front of me, Dan begins.

"He got hooked on this idea about orange. Here's what he was saying (Dan reads from a scrap of paper): *I'm not going to (he stops, looks away). On the second day, the second coming is coming, by God. Orange is inside God, God isn't yellow, He likes oranges. He made them all; after all, God is God. My hands are turning orange and my body is going on exhibit at the l'Orangerie.* This might not be verbatim, but it's close, it's very close to that. Words repeat a lot and he jumps from one thing to another. It is as if everything he says is perfectly sensible and obvious."

I smile at him, because I do catch the drift of this kind of speaking. Dan has said it very well, and he hears this kind of speech repeatedly because he visits his brother weekly.

"Who speaks here?" I ask Dan. "This is not your brother, as you've known him?"

Dan shakes his head, "That's the problem. This doesn't sound like David at all!"

"Why not?"

"David, the old David, doesn't rhyme like this, and repeat things. He does know French, but he was never very religious. And, well, he doesn't seem to be speaking to me."

"Yes," I agree, "David is not speaking to you, his brother. The 'you' here could be anyone at all. He has lost the place of a personal address in his speech. And it seems as if he can't find words in language that work *as language*."

Dan looks confused, "Yes, but what kind of language is he using then?"

"Lacan called unfinished statements 'message phenomena' [Lacan, 2006, p. 452]. There is an anticipated meaning in the sentence that concerns the subject, or his experience, but that gets suspended, and can't be finished."

"Oh," Dan says. "Yeah, he said, *I'm not going to*, and he just stopped, and looked away. I didn't know if he was going to come back to that, but he didn't."

"Maybe that's a problem for him, to know and to say what he refuses," I offer.

"Yeah, I can imagine that. We are really not listening to him any more."

"For what it's worth, Lacan suggested we listen for *a protest* in what seem to be foreign elements in speech, even neologisms. These are clues to what the person is trying to say, but can't say."

"A protest?" Dan asks.

"Yes. The psychotic will speak what bits of language are imposed on him, and it can sound somewhat incoherent. Sometimes there is a protest, but it's hard to hear that."

"I'm thinking. He said a lot about orange. Maybe he's been eating oranges, or orange foods," Dan laughs. "And he said, 'God isn't yellow'! The only protest is that allusion to something he's not going to do?" Dan pauses.

"And his body is going on exhibit at the l'Orangerie?" I ask.

"Yeah. David knows French, has been to France, so he said that."

"He's not going, and he's going—it repeats," I notice.

"But none of it makes any sense. There's no meaning here!" Dan says, and sighs.

I speak softly, "David might feel that some parts of his own speech are foreign to him, puzzling to him. *He* might not know what he means! Psychotic speaking is an address that does not signify the subject. What I mean is that what is *really at issue*, really at stake, can't be articulated. He can't say what is most crucial. In place of that, your brother produces an Other speaking, as if words, phrases, were moving through him, as pure enigma. Lacan [2006] called these elements that are imposed and foreign to the speaker 'code phenomena' [p. 450]. David is talking about things that matter to him, or else he wouldn't bother to speak. He sounds confused, but words repeat, and, you know, you can ask him questions, wait for responses."

Dan puts his head in his hands. "I don't know him any more; I don't know *what* he is saying, or *how* to ask him."

I wonder what to I can say to Dan. I decide to just go with what is streaming through my mind: "If you treat him as though you can't hear him, or can't understand *anything*, if you listen to him as though what he says has no merit, you will learn nothing, and, after a time, he might not even bother to try to speak when you are around."

I wait, to give Dan time to take this in.

"But, if you treat him as someone who is trying to speak, has to say something to you, and you ask questions, and make guesses (that you ask him to correct, to clarify, sooner or later, he might say something he wants to say, and that is like happening on a little island of lucidity. Then he addresses you, Dan, his brother, if only for a moment. You are the witness to what he is experiencing."

Dan's eyes fill. What more can I say? He rises, turns away, and pets the cat.

And now? Three months after my last visit with Dan, his brother is living with his parents again. He's joined a day treatment programme and entered into psychotherapy. He takes a low dose of Clozaril. Dan has had some success in speaking with his brother again, but it is still hard to understand him. Dan persists.

I sit in my office at Austen Riggs in the aftermath of a blizzard, wondering again about Dan's question: "What is it, this strangeness?" He does not presume to know. We spoke of so many things. Yet, I wonder, did we get to the heart of his brother's suffering? Probably not. I doubt that we got even close.

When I think about Dan, who he is and what he is doing, I feel some hope for his brother. Dan sought me out because he knew he was losing David, did not understand what was happening to him, and could not find a way to reach him. Dan wanted to think about his brother's experience in relation to his own, and find a way to grasp what was, truthfully, an unthinkable terrain. And he persists in listening, gathering David into a small social link of two, in the face of no easy answers and an uncertain future.

To my ear, David's speech carries his unique relation to language and meaning. The holes in his speech, as well as the repetitions and circular logic, are the signatures of *incandescent alphabets*—a new language that emerges with psychosis to speak about things that have no place in the social link or conventional language.

In the next two chapters, I explore these incandescent alphabets through images of the body, as well as invented codes, alphabets, musical notations, geometries, scripts, and illegible scribbles, all made by artists living in psychosis.

CHAPTER THREE

Hallucinated bodies: art and its alphabets in psychosis

"Who, if I cried, would hear me among the Angelic
Orders? And even if one of them suddenly
took me to its heart, I would fade in the strength of its
stronger existence. For beauty is nothing
but the beginning of terror we are just still able to bear
. . . Every single Angel is terrible"

(Rilke, First Elegy, *Duino Elegies*, 1939)

I have drawn since I was a child: my baseball mitt, the sycamore trees behind our apartment, my cat, my own hands, and maps, make-believe ideas of place. Near the end of high school, following nine months in a psychiatric hospital and a diagnosis of schizophrenia, I found that I could not draw in perspective; something was "off" in my seeing that inhabited my drawing. The St Louis Cathedral did not resemble my memory of it from outside, so I drew the architecture of its vastness as though I could see through it, into its interior workings. In my first year college drawing class, I discovered an incomprehensible gap between the nude bodies of our models and what I started to draw on paper, a body I can only call terrible. I was filled with

45

dread, and dropped the class. Four months later I was back in a psychiatric hospital.

As I turn to writing about the art of psychotic patients I cannot go about it any other way but in pieces, gathered to evoke rather than to explain. I veer from the vertigo of looking at images to writing about my experience of seeing and wondering. What is the body inhabited by and taken over by something strange, filled with dread? The body: a terrifying beauty.

Each day, I study images of the body made by psychotic artists. I begin with a collection made by Hans Prinzhorn, a German psychiatrist who also trained as an art historian and archived works made by patients living in the early twentieth century. I know little about many of the artists. My purpose here is not to review the work of Prinzhorn, its scope and reach, nor its controversy. I am not seeking biographical particularities or interpretations so much as psychotic signatures in art, incandescent alphabets of the body—what it is, how it works—as I view and respond to these stunning images.

Whatever we can name and recognise of ourselves in language becomes a precursor for what we see and experience about our bodies.

When language itself comes from voices imposed, the body becomes marked by the problematic of an invasion. The artist makes an expanding projection of unspeakable experience. As we look, the horizon between the image created and the world experienced comes towards us. The artists portray what we have not seen before. The body becomes fragmented; it has too many organs or has lost vital organs; it is made transparent; foreign objects control the body; the body is reinscribed to support a new universe, a new humanity.

The artists present singular works that speak to anyone who wonders about psychosis as a lived experience, anyone who believes in the power of art. As I write this chapter and choose these images, I am constructing a series of visual moments. Intentionally, I keep my responses brief, and intersperse them with quotations that adumbrate what I am seeing and seeking. This is a poetics I am making in relation to the images, a layer of impressions.

The images are beyond interpretation; they live on the page in the way they affect us, disturb us, and render us as children, small and unknowing.

The body: a terrifying beauty

I begin with a picture by Joseph Forster (Image 1).

Image 1. Joseph Forster, *Untitled*, 1916–1921, Inv. No. 4494.
© Prinzhorn Collection, University Hospital Heidelberg.

Forster was a paper-hanger, diagnosed schizophrenic. I know almost nothing about him. Yet, his image speaks to me beyond his life and across a century of time.

Forster's body floats, grounded only by his hands holding on to long poles, his mouth invisible and muffled with a scarf. The blue of the scarf repeats in the blue of one sock. The body moves though space, over a field. It seems to walk on air, while the poles walk on the ground, a paradox. Is it there, this paradox, or do I project it into the space of looking?

The next image is by Paul Goesch, an architect, diagnosed schizophrenic, who was killed by the Nazis in 1940 (Image 2).

Can a body, dismembered, float or swim? Impossible. There are two small figures standing on the water in the upper right corner. They are intact, but faded, and do not take up much space in the picture frame. Whatever it is that has intervened with the body has made crude cuts that mark the neck, the torso's arm and leg sockets, and one of the arms. The body parts still work; they seem to float in opposite directions within the multiple shapes of an "O". Each "O"

Image 2. Paul Goesch, *Horus dismembered*, undated, Inv. No. 881.
© Prinzhorn Collection, University Hospital Heidelberg.

has three arches, surely not an accident for a trained architect? I think of this letter and what it contains as an incandescent alphabet for what is unspeakable.

The body: a record of what it is, a series of impossibilities made Real.

The body: an intervention, what has intervened, and how it is working now.

The body: on which something was written, imposed as a new alphabet, enigmatic.

I am taking the bus home from a suburb of the city on a grey winter day. I look outside to see the street filled with water, churning. How will the bus go through it? It moves with seeming ease. I look again: legs, arms, heads, detached in the river of water, yet living, moving in the water. My body readjusts to *what it is*—it is outside the bus while inside the bus. Outside, in pieces in cold water, churning, and at the same time inside, a nineteen-year-old girl holding a stack of books on her lap going home to her dinner.

A particular time: in the late 1800s and into the first two decades of the 1900s. The time before antipsychotic medications and their effects (damping down both symptoms and a sense of being fully alive), when one might live in an asylum all one's life. A particular person: Hans Prinzhorn, a psychiatrist then working in Heidelberg, who begins to collect the art of the patients, and ask them about making it. In *The Artistry of the Mentally Ill* (1972[1922]), he writes of a striking trend in art by schizophrenic patients: "Human figures are outlined by forceful and complicated looped strokes" (p. 63).

Now we have the image by Jacob Mohr (Image 3). Mohr was a farmer, a gardener, diagnosed paranoid.

The arrows of his image seem to move in one direction, towards the figure on the hill. Yet, the arrows infiltrate the ground and both bodies. The cursive script on the right side and the horizon writes on the sky, on the body.

What changes in the body in the face of an encounter, relentless, of an invasion of voices? Lacan called this experience Real *jouissance*, an energy running in the body, unbound. What breaks into the body is Other, strange; this Otherness, this strangeness *becomes* the body. I cannot read the words written around the drawing by Jacob Mohr. The drawing of electric currents rewrites the body and what it is; the body can be controlled and re-made. The forms of electricity repeat. Is

Image 3. Jacob Mohr, *Proofs*, 1910, Inv. No. 627/1 recto.
© Prinzhorn Collection, University Hospital Heidelberg.

it illogical, the iteration of marks to the point of no point at all, or another logic in which every mark counts?

Here is August Natterer speaking about his art:

> At first I saw a white spot in a cloud, very near by—the clouds all stood still—then the white spot withdrew and remained in the sky the whole time, like a board. On this board or screen or stage pictures followed one another like lightening . . . They are pictures like those of which Christ spoke. They are revealed to me by God for the completion of the redemption. (Prinzhorn, 1972[1922], pp. 159–160)

From the notes on Natterer's admission, Prinzhorn summarises:

> It seemed as if a broom were sweeping inside his chest and stomach; his skin had turned into fur; his bones and throat were petrified; in his stomach he has a tree trunk; his blood consisted of water, animals came out of his nose. He sees the devil in the shape of a column of fire perform dances in front of him; poems about him appear in newspapers; he is the AntiChrist, the genuine one; he must live forever, he could not die. He no longer has a heart; his soul has been torn out. He explains the cracking in his knees as telephone calls by which the devil down below is always notified of his whereabouts. (Prinzhorn, 1972[1922], p. 160)

Signification passes to the psychotic subject through an Other as direct message, and even if that meaning is perplexing, it is directed and emanates *significance*. Natterer is eloquent about what he sees and hears, what he is subjected to, and what he experiences in his body: a fantastic and endless torment.

Who is this Other? Where is he, and what does he want from me?

What is the significance of what the Other imposes on me, beyond my control?

What speaks to me, taking over my thoughts, inhabiting my body?

"The subject's relation of exteriority to the signifier is so striking that all clinicians have emphasized it in one way or another" (Lacan, 1997[1981], p. 250).

"Marks are the alphabets that form the words that make the prose, and are the elements with which the drawing is made. It is the gestural language of drawing" (Maslen & Southern, 2011, p. 28).

"There is an invitation to make our own rebus from the elements, a narrative sentence from the different pieces" (Kentridge, 2014, p. 134).

What were these men and women doing in the asylum? They were drawing, drawing and painting, making marks that carried their very gestures. They were making new visual alphabets, too. They drew, and left a rebus of works, the elements of psychosis portrayed as distinctive signatures.

Most surely, they were artists.

The sea, if it is the sea, this vast aqua blue? (Image 4).

Image 4. August Natterer (pseudonym Neter), *The Miraculous Shepherd*,
1911–1917, Inv. No. 176.
© Prinzhorn Collection, University Hospital Heidelberg.

The sea. A shepherd stands holding a staff, looking out, accompanied by a little dog. The shepherd stands on a snake, or perhaps it is an arm of the figure that seems to rise out of the ocean, a fish head and a human head, hair flayed out wide. If it is human, it is also lying on top of the water, one leg a vertical in the air, the foot a little awning over the shepherd and the snake biting his hat. Or does its mouth simply define the shape of the hat? The other leg extends in a horizontal with an opening, vaginal perhaps, no, perhaps a bone, a spine, attached to a transparent foot that extends into the body of the head emerging. It is virtually impossible to describe this image in prose. It is a new alphabet of the body. Only poetry approximates this.

"Registers the murmurs of speed, the miniscule terror, searches under some cold cinders for the smallest birds, those which never close their wings, resist the wind" (Eluard, 1981, p. 3).

August Natterer, an electrician, married, without a diagnosis, dies in the Rottwell Asylum. Natterer also made art designed to reconfigure time and the cosmos.

Looking: the artist makes an expanding projection of unspeakable experience.

Looking: the horizon between the image created and the world experienced comes towards us.

HERE IT HAPPENED.

HERE IS THE POINT OF GREATEST PARADOX.

HERE A VOICE INVADED THE MIND AND REMOULDED THE BODY.

HERE IS HOW IT WORKS.

Image 5 is by Hyacinth Freiherr von Wieser.

Suddenly, there is this transparency of the head, of the mind. A baroque theatre of planes and angles, wound up with a little key extending from the left side, and a larger key from the left shoulder. An incomprehensible confusion; it erases him, his face, his thoughts. And then this dazed thing without armour. The man who drew this image had a doctorate in Law. In his youth he had written poems, plays, and short stories.

"We who draw do so not only to make something visible to others, but also to accompany something invisible to its incalculable destination" (Berger, 2011, p. 9).

August Natterer painted heads, too. Space flattens under the gaze of the head depicted in Image 6, the eye an orb, unseeing all-seeing

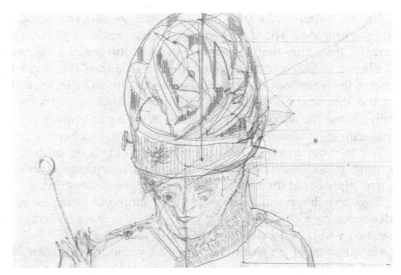

Image 5. Hyacinth Freiherr von Wieser (pseudonym Welz), *Power Idea View*,
undated, Inv. No. 2457.
© Prinzhorn Collection, University Hospital Heidelberg.

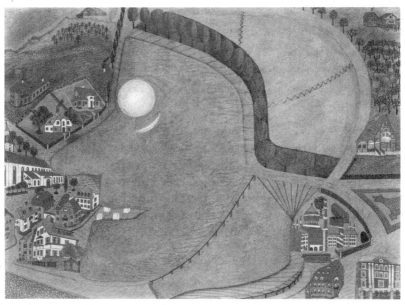

Image 6. August Natterer (pseudonym Neter), *Witch's Head*, before 1920,
Inv. No. 184.
© Prinzhorn Collection, University Hospital Heidelberg.

void. The head dominates the entire world of the image, and the world, its buildings and streets, the surrounding woods, come into a strange, distorted perspective. It is hard to know if the head is dead or alive. The gaze is not just uncomfortable; it is uncanny, persecutory.

The body remakes the world; the eye opens on to a void and gives a glimpse of horror. The voices—sounding, resounding—speak over and remake the body. The head becomes a gateway to a new universe, its eyes and its ears open to vistas others do not see, cannot hear, and do not want to know.

Cosmic body

Image 7 is by Aloïse Corbaz, diagnosed schizophrenic.

This image of multiple women embedded in women, the largest lying down across two pages, several with halos and wings, is a re-envisioning of the Magi, the three kings who came to visit Christ. Aloïse Corbaz was a prolific artist at the La Rosiere asylum, where she died at age seventy-eight. Her psychiatrist, Dr Jacqueline Porret-Forel, spoke with Aloïse about her art.

> Aloïse's work is based on her own cosmic vision; the universe became her family; impregnated by the light of the sun, she was transmuted into a creator from whom any being might arise. She saw no inconsistency in remaining herself and at the same time becoming a ubiquitous, eternal other. She lived in a world turned upside down, propping the heavens with her feet and standing upright on a celestial carpet. She played with the stars, tossed the terrestrial globe into space and rejuvenated it. She never looked back. Her work is a cosmic theatre in which she saw herself as demiurge. (Ferrier, 1998, pp. 117–118)

Here, the human body reconfigures the cosmos. Whatever is wrong with the Other, a defect in the universe that has returned and imposed itself in the Real of the body, the subject of psychosis tries to fix that flaw. This is a bodily experience in which the "I" becomes vast, as the body is remoulded to support a new universe or a new humanity. Religious motifs put to some idiosyncratic use no longer belong to collective belief, but are part of the artist's singular vision.

Image 7. Aloïse Corbaz, *Adoration des Mages petit palais de Grenoble*, 1941, mine de plomb et crayon de couleur sur papier, 25 x 66 cm. Photo: Amélie Blanc, Atelier de numérisation, Ville de Lausanne. Collection de l'Art Brut, Lausanne, no inv. cab-9396.

Body effaced

Else Blankenhorn made notebooks in the years following her diagnosis of catatonia (Image 8).

The figures, if they are human figures, have no features; any identifying detail has been effaced.

Just as the body becomes enlarged to fill the cosmos, so may it disappear into a schematic semblance of a human figure.

Foreign object in the body

Image 9 is by Robert Gie, diagnosed with persecution mania with hallucinations, who resided at Rosegg Hospital.

This image, translated *Circulation of Effluvia with Central Machine and Metric Scale*, portrays the Other in the body, the effects of something foreign imposed and working in the body. It is the visual counterpart to voices overwriting one's thoughts.

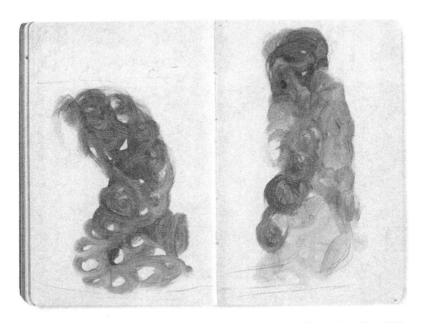

Image 8.   Else Blankenhorn, *Poetry Album with Drawings and Texts*, Inv. No. 4318a.
© Prinzhorn Collection, University Hospital Heidelberg.

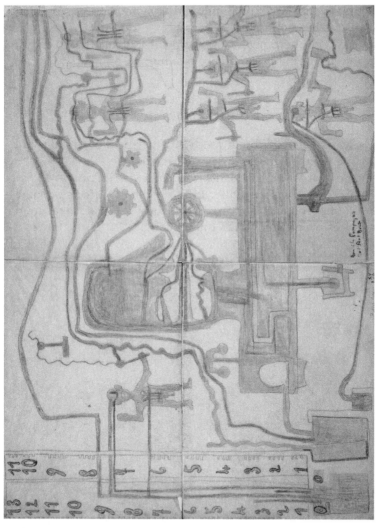

Image 9. Robert Gie, *Distribution d'effluves avec machine centrale et tableau métrique*, ca 1916, mine de plomb et crayon de couleur sur papier, 49 x 69 cm.
Photo: Arnaud Conne, Atelier de numérisation, Ville de Lausanne, Collection de l'Art Brut, Lausanne, no inv. cab–A419.

The body proliferates, dehumanised, automated, remote-controlled by means of a foreign object in the stomach or abdomen of each figure; the human traversed by mysterious fluids or currents.

The body as destiny

Camille Caudel exhibited the figure depicted in Image 10 at the Paris Salon in 1893. Clotho, the youngest of the Three Fates, was responsible for spinning the thread of human life, determining the fate of all humans.

Image 10.   Camille Claudel, *Clotho*, numéro d'inventaire S.1379, Plâtre, 90 x 49.50 x 43.50 cm.
Photograph by Christian Baraja, Musée Rodin, Paris.

Along with her sisters and the god Hermes, Clotho created the Greek alphabet.

"I have fallen into an abyss. I live in a world so curious, so strange. Of the dream that was my life, this is my nightmare" (Claudel, quoted in Ayral-Clause, 2002, p. 9).

Following her father's death, Claudel was committed to the mental asylum at Ville-Évrard. She accused Rodin of having had her committed so as to get his hands on her works, and became strikingly paranoid, even afraid to eat her food. During the Second World War, she was transferred to the asylum at Montdevergues, where she remained until her death in 1943 (Ayral-Clause, 2002).

". . . his haggard, boney, bearded face, peering through diamond panes, cries out" (Joyce, 2010[1922], p. 472) (Image 11).

Image 11.   Franz Karl Bühler, *Untitled*, 1909–1916, Inv. No. 2939.
© Prinzhorn Collection, University Hospital Heidelberg,

I look at this face and marvel at its form and layers. A face with the ears of an animal, a third eye, a metal hat or a plate, perhaps—yet the face is recognisably human with its thin nose, intent eyes, and the hint of a smile. The throat seems open, raw and transparent, but perhaps it is only a scarf I am seeing.

Franz Bühler, a metalworker and lecturer diagnosed schizophrenic, was killed by the Nazis in 1940, his madness, whatever it was, overtaken by a collective madness.

The body in pieces: missing organs and disjointed parts

Antonin Artaud, 1896–1948, was a French poet, playwright, theorist, actor and theatre director, perhaps best known for his work, *The Theatre and Its Double* (1958). Diagnosed schizophrenic in May 1937, he spent nine years in mental institutions. He drew and wrote in notebooks, documented in *50 Drawings to Murder Magic*, translated into English in 2008 (Image 12).

"No mouth/no tongue/no teeth/no larynx/no esophagus/no stomach/no intestine/no anus" (Artaud, quoted in Deleuze, 1993 [1969], p. 101).

> There are the trees peculiarly fixed here and there. And there are sudden forest fires. And on the summit of the mounts, there is the ozone of a digestive electricity, that was never anything for me but the stomach of all the pulverized, lost bodies. (Artaud in Heller-Roazen, 2007)

Artaud wrote the lines quoted above to his physician from the village of Espalion, twenty miles from the Rodez Hospital.

> The body without organs is an egg: it is crisscrossed with axes and thresholds, with latitudes and longitudes and geodesic lines, traversed by gradients marking the transitions and the becomings, the destinations of the subject developing along these particular vectors. (Deleuze & Guattari, 2004[1972], p. 19)

"There looms, within abjection, one of those violent, dark revolts of being" (Julia Kristeva, quoted in Olivier, 2009, p. 153).

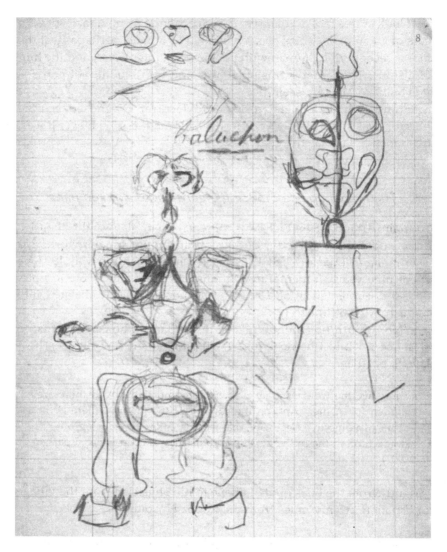

Image 12.   Antonin Artaud, *Drawing #36*, Exercise book 351 (August, 1947).
© 2015 Artists Rights Society (ARS), New York/ADAGP, Paris.

What is it that carves out the very organs of the body and carries them off? The body is in exile, cut into pieces by language itself, as both Freud and Lacan recognised. "The body is contrasted from the organism insofar as it is the body that is spoken of (*un corps parlé*), carved up and made visible by language" (Apollon et al., 2002, p. 36).

In psychosis, invented language re-carves a new body.

The heterogeneous body

The psychotic finds himself without organs, but also, at times, with too many.

The figures in Image 13 are by Karl Genzel.

Karl Genzel, once a bricklayer and ironworker, spoke about these figures to Hans Prinzhorn (1972[1922]): "One of them committed sin with Sabbedaus behind the altar" (p. 115). He described ". . . a whole radio station in his body . . . stabbing and tickling in his body, especially the genitals; his food tastes of all kinds of chemicals, mostly poisons" (p. 105). Genzel wrote hundreds of pages in his notebooks. He wrote the excerpt on the following page in June, 1912:

Image 13.   Karl Genzel (pseudonym Brendel) *Three Head and Feet Figurines*:
(a) Karl Genzel, "The Woman with the Stork" or "Jesin" (Cephalopod),
undated, Inv. No. 122, (b) Karl Genzel, "Jesus on the Ship",
before 1920, Inv. No. 150/17, (c) Karl Genzel, "The Woman with the
Elephant Feet" or "Jesus" (Cephalopod), Wood, undated, Inv. No. 123.
© Prinzhorn Collection, University Hospital Heidelberg.

Heavenhell in subterranean ground of deepfession. One pumps out the head through lightening thunder hail . . . whirl through howl over nut South East North West through ball snake sing in the visibility with that came Herscht Ahtrobant Light who heareth the groaning in the glow body . . . searchlight in syllables . . . (Prinzhorn, 1972[1922]), p. 99)

The body of the psychotic becomes open to every kind of fantasmic capture by the Other. He cannot identify as a man, she as a woman. The question of sexual existence meets an impossible Real that the artist renders in the Imaginary, making an image both animal and human, a human being with the organs of both sexes. This art repeats the structure of hallucination—an experience of enigma and strangeness that imposes a new order and an incandescent alphabet, a synthesis of hearing and seeing things that do not exist collectively: "searchlight in syllables".

Henry Darger, born in 1892, lost his mother and his sister, and was taken from his father as a child. As a teenager, Darger ran away from a residential school for "feeble-minded" children, walking back to his native Chicago. He lived for decades in a small room on the north side of the city, working as a janitor. He did not speak to those who addressed him, but kept company (aloud) with voices in his room. Wandering the streets and alleyways of Chicago, he collected newspapers and magazines and saved his money for art supplies: children's paints, glue, colouring books, and later, photographic copies of images. He drew and painted children, girls with testicles and penises, girls who are part animal, with wings and horns, in fantasmic landscapes, sometimes on panels twelve feet wide (MacGregor, 2002). Darger borrowed his images from colouring books and magazines from his time. Darger's Vivian girls, girls at war and under threat of slavery and death, witness catastrophes at the hands of adults. On the next page they are tormented, bloodied, hanged (Image 14).

Only a few of us, amid the great fabrications of society, hang on to our really childish reactions, still wonder naively what we are doing on the earth and what sort of joke is being played on us. We want to decipher skies and paintings, go behind these starry backgrounds or these painted canvases and, like kids trying to find a gap in a fence, try to look through the cracks in the world. One of these cracks is the cruel custom of sacrifice. (Bataille, 1988[1949], p.2)

Image 14.   Henry Darger, *At Norma Catherine via Jennie Richie. Vivian girls witness*
              children's bowels and other entrails torn out by infuriated Glandelinians.
              Left panel of three panel collage-drawing, watercolor, pencil,
              carbon on paper, 22 x 89 in. c 1988. Henry Darger:
              © 2015 Kiyoko Lerner/Artists Rights Society (ARS), New York.

Darger's art integrates a marvellous accumulation of images. His figures fill panels, some taped together in a continuous vision twelve to fifteen feet wide. His girls flock, run, and cluster together in fantastic panoramas (Image 15).

> A great plane flew across the sun
> And the girls ran along the ground . . .
> Surging over her shoulder like a wave of energy, and then—
> It was gone. No one had witnessed it but herself.
>
> (Ashbery, 1999, pp. 3–4)

I read John Ashbery's long poem, *Girls on the Run* (1999), alongside *Henry Darger: In the Realms of the Unreal* (2002), a compilation of reproductions of Darger's art and writing, as well as research into his life by John MacGregor. I discovered the latter book in the north side of Chicago in the Intuit Museum, where I first encountered Darger's

Image 15.   Henry Darger, *At Jennie Richie. After being shown how to escape from Guern by their help, they ask the creatures to display their wings, which they do.* Collage, watercolor, and carbon tracing on pieced paper. Private Collection. Henry Darger: © 2015 Kiyoko Lerner/Artists Rights Society (ARS), New York.

work. I also travelled to New York, to see his larger paintings in the American Folk Museum, and to visit the Darger archive in Brooklyn to view the process he used to make his art.

Darger's life work had been private, entirely private. His landlord, also an artist, found a vast project in Darger's room shortly before his death in 1973. Darger had written the history of another world in fifteen volumes: *In the Realms of the Unreal.* The writing comprised 15,145 type written pages, and told the story of seven sisters, "the Vivian Girls", who were in a prolonged, violent conflict with adults over child enslavement on another planet. There were three huge volumes of coloured illustrations, many created as collages, and some painted on both sides. Some panels spanned more than twelve feet across, extraordinary when I consider the confines of his single small room. Henry Darger lived most of his life outside an asylum or hospital. Whether he was a visionary artist, or an undiagnosed psychotic, his art attests to a life-long commitment to a work that evokes an

Other of torment, catastrophe, and horror as well as great beauty and wonder.

I walk down the street from my office on the Austen Riggs campus, past cottages and out to Main Street in Stockbridge, past St Paul's church on my left and the Red Lion Inn on my right to "The Lavender Door", a space dedicated to art in an "interpretation free" zone for the Riggs patients. On the lintel over the door, I see Artaud's words. "No one has ever written, painted, sculpted, modeled, built, or invented except literally to get out of hell" (Artaud, 1976).

I go up to the second floor, through the theatre set, and find Mark Mulherrin in a spacious art studio flooded with light. He is alone and free to talk with me. He, too, has an interest in psychotic art. I tell him about my book and some of my impressions of the art. He lends me his copies of art books and a contemporary journal, *Raw Vision* (2012). Mark tells me that he does not collect art journals—but *this* kind of art, art of psychotics, or visionaries, or outsiders, whatever that means, speaks to him. The artists are daring; they make images others will not, perhaps cannot, make. As we sit and talk, I learn that the images I have been looking at and wondering about have infiltrated the art world, and now appear in auctions, galleries, and museums. Professional non-psychotic artists aspire to this art, and make art that is very like it, if not copies of it.

It was Jean Dubuffet, the creator of the term "art brut" in the mid-1940s, who created a cultural change in the way we read, receive, and value art from artists who are mentally ill or psychotic. He wrote, "Art does not come and lie in the beds we make for it. It slips away as soon as its name is uttered; it likes to preserve its incognito. Its best moments are when it forgets its name" (Thevoz, 1995, p. 11).

I wonder, in the present context, whether or not psychotics still make art that "forgets its name"—extending, illuminating elements of "delusion"—revealed to them through the "symptoms" of madness. Have antipsychotic medications damped down or changed the extraordinary art we saw from the time before these medications were introduced? As I search the web for art made by psychotics, I see that they inhabit a different world than their predecessors in asylums of the past century. Some artists call themselves visionary while others identify as schizophrenic. Some have attended art schools while others have not, and many are connected to galleries or art collectives. I am glad to see their work live in the world of artists.

I chose Dwight Mackintosh because his images spoke to me as singular and connected to writing, as if the body itself were inscribed with something new. His drawings opened up a contemporary counterpoint to the art made at the turn of the last century in this chapter.

Born in Haywood, California in 1906, at sixteen Mackintosh entered an institution for the mentally retarded. His records speculate about his diagnosis: post natal brain injury, mental retardation, and mental illness. After fifty-six years, in 1978, the deinstitutionalisation of the mentally ill resulted in his release at the age of seventy-two. His brother Earl brought him to visit the Creative Growth Art Center in Oakland, California. Mackintosh was given drawing materials and immediately began drawing. Each day, this withdrawn, isolated, and almost non-verbal man spent hours absorbed in the process of drawing. From the beginning he approached each drawing with complete certainty. He drew for more than twenty years, and died in 1999 following a stroke (creativegrowth.org).

"Every production of an artist should be the expression of an adventure of his soul" (Maugham, 1992[1938] p. 310).

But what is art—and how do we read its "expression"—after decades in an institution?

What was Mackintosh thinking as he drew, as he wrote? And was he writing something to be read? I do not know. Throughout his twenty-year art-making career, two elements defined his work: powerful intertwining lines that formed figures and unintelligible writing. In the writing, fragments of words can sometimes be discerned, "i's" are dotted, "t's" are crossed. Text often begins with a capital "D" and ends with "ich", suggestive of his name (Image 16). Is this a signature? Mackintosh was never willing or able to translate his writing (MacGregor, 1990).

Four figures float in space. Contour lines define the interior torus of bodies, faces, hands, feet, and large penises. Above these intricate figures the text floats, word-like and unreadable. In this image I read, again, the incandescent alphabets of an Imaginary body; a new language of seeing, drawing, and considering what it is to be human.

The body: a record of what it is, a series of impossibilities made Real.

The body: on which something was written, imposed as a new alphabet, enigmatic.

The body: an unnamed animal (Image 17).

Image 16.   Dwight Mackintosh, *Untitled* (Four full-length male figures), 1983,
Pencil, chalk and watercolour, 40 x 26 in.
Permanent Collection, Creative Growth Art Center, Oakland.
Image courtesy of Creative Growth Art Center.

The title "outsider artist" has made a space for artists to be taken seriously, exhibited, acknowledged in public spaces. I am glad of that. But it is much more difficult to identify the art of those who are psychotic, and have lived through that distinctive human experience.

As I read the images made by men and women in asylums, as well as those who created art and yet lived profoundly isolated lives (both Darger and Mackintosh), I wondered about the writing that so often accompanied these images. The writing appears to me as part of the drawings themselves. What is this writing?

Writing in and around images—what is it?

A new language for what has never been spoken, never been seen?

A script that has forgotten how to speak its own name?

A search for a missing code?

> *Spaces one cannot enter*
> *Figures one cannot reconcile*
> *Objects one cannot use*
> *Text one cannot read*

Image 17.   Dwight Mackintosh, *Untitled* (Animal), 1985, Felt pen, chalk and
watercolour, 15 x 26 in. Permanent Collection, Creative Growth Art
Center, Oakland. Image courtesy of Creative Growth Art Center.

Many of the artists in this chapter died in an asylum. We would
not have their art but for the collections made by those who saw it,
and knew it *was* art. None of these men and women, to my knowledge, had access to psychoanalysis, or made it back to lucidity and
entered life again as full citizens of the world. Yet, their art is stun-
ningly revelatory of an experience we still fail to grasp and to respect:
the experience of invasion by a ghastly, perverse Other from which
there is no escape. Their art is a testimony that this experience changes
language and what it does, the body and what it is, into incandescent
alphabets.

I am of this lineage. I lived in psychosis for almost two decades,
and did not get the formal art training that I wanted. But I persisted
in making images: sketches, paintings, and prints. Following psycho-

analysis, I do not have access to the visionary worlds of these artists; my words speak to other listeners, and it matters to me to be heard in a collective. I work at Zea Mays Printmaking, an artists' print studio in Western Massachusetts, where I play a part in conversations, decisions, ideas about shows and public events. In my notebooks, images unfold accompanied by phrases and lines of poetry, words that speak in relation to the images, a joyful rendering of whimsical impossibilities (Image 18).

Image 18.   Annie Rogers, *Untitled*, Pencil and pen, Moleskin Notebook, 2011.

CHAPTER FOUR

Infinite code: clocks, calendars, numbers, music, scripts

I n his novel, *The Unnamable*, Samuel Beckett creates a first person voice floundering with questions of identity, voice, and knowledge. Perplexity empties this character of all but "the voices and thoughts of the devils who beset me" (Beckett, 1994[1951], p. 350). Beckett's readers cannot escape pervasive perplexity.

> Is there a single word of mine in all I say? No, I have no voice, in this matter I have none. That's one of the reasons I confused myself with Worm. But I have no reasons, either no reason, I'm like Worm, without voice or reason, I'm Worm, no, if I were Worm I wouldn't know it, I wouldn't say it, I wouldn't say anything, I'd be Worm. But I don't say anything, I don't know anything, these voices are not mine, nor these thoughts, but the voices and thoughts of the devils who beset me. (p. 350)

Hallucination, for Lacan, is not a perception without an object; rather, the object has an effect on the subject who experiences it as external, yet intimate and deeply puzzling. What invades the mind as a voice or presence is strange and foreign, inescapable, a part of oneself and yet not oneself, ejected from meaning. The effect is perplexity. Here is a message; what is the code needed to grasp it?

Language changes in psychosis. Words become the floating signifiers of a mad Other who takes up a place in speech. Speech elements connect to nothing, have no meaning whatsoever, and disrupt the meaning that was unfolding. These elements, whether heard or spoken, drawn or written, are foreign to the speaker, and create a profound sense of disorder with respect to speaking.

She cannot find her place in language. He questions if his thoughts are actually his, and concludes they are not. How is it possible then to orientate oneself in language? Language becomes a puzzling body of signs, bewildering signs without a code or key. Artists in psychosis make clocks, calendars, numbers, music, and scripts, the infinite unfolding of code, emerging incandescent alphabets.

August Natterer, the artist of *The Miraculous Shepherd* in Chapter Three, envisioned "the clock of the world running backward", and said of it, "since the clock of the world is running down and going backward, its hands are always running forward in order to delude the people of the disorder of the works inside" (Prinzhorn, 1972[1922], p. 161). While the clock of the world is running backwards (revealed knowledge), the clock hands run forward to "delude the people about disorder of the works inside" (and only the subject knows this). Time, like language, does not work. Something Other creates disorder in time (Image 19).

And what to do with time then? Order it.

Prinzhorn (1972[1922]) comments, "Neter [Natterer] claimed that the whole picture [*World Axis and Rabbit*] has predicted the World War—he had known everything in advance, including the end of the war" (p. 168). Prinzhorn adds, "Everything he says and does betrays a certain discipline, an almost objective logic, in practical matters as well as the delusional system" (p. 162).

A delusional system creates an order, but delusion itself is subjected to destabilising *new* foreign speech elements in psychosis. In this sense, delusion is always a work in progress.

Lacan argued that delusion is not a false belief, because it is not a belief at all. Delusion is built under a new order of linguistic elements. Some speech elements are foreign to the speaker yet perceived as *significant*; they are not evaluated as personal beliefs at all. These elements float, without reference to other meanings, as *autonyms* (Vanheule, 2011). Since they are *revealed* to the subject and come as elements outside her own beliefs, she cannot question whether *or not* to believe them.

Image 19.   August Natterer (pseudonym Neter), *World Axis and Rabbit*, 1911, Inv. No.157. © Prinzhorn Collection, University Hospital Heidelberg.

In the face of such a pervasive change in language, the psychotic subject, confounded by non-sense, begins to create a proto-order with connotations of a linguistic order. The proto-order, however, does not signify the position of the subject, what she thinks or feels or wants or knows.

Lacan observes that the psychotic experiences a negative form of the imposed speech elements; suddenly there is no thought, no word, as if one's very thoughts have been stolen. When God withdraws from Schreber, he is at a complete loss, and turns to counting. To count is to restore a working metonymy, a form of signification that orders time, sequences, or elements.

Does this order not signify the position of the subject with respect to what is happening to him, if we could only render it readable?

Yet, as I look at these works that depict ordering systems, they read as private codes (Image 20).

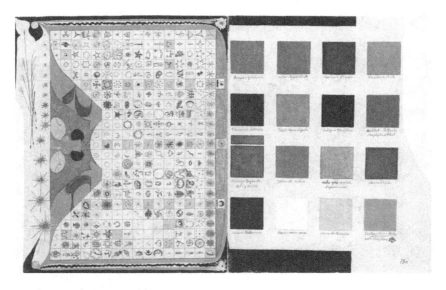

Image 20.   Joseph Heinrich Grebing, *Untitled*, before 1920, Inv. No. 624/12.
© Prinzhorn Collection, University Hospital Heidelberg.

Joseph Grebing was a Catholic shopkeeper, committed in 1906 to the Heidelberg Psychiatric Clinic, his diagnosis dementia praecox.

He made colour charts, chronologies, and a calendar of executioners and murderers. All around him was danger. He tried to grasp it with an all-embracing cosmological system.

Ironically, Grebing *was* in danger; he was taken and killed by the Nazis in 1940, as were many others living in asylums at that time.

Grebing made sheets of numbers and letters in different coloured inks, crossed out some tiny part at the bottom, and began again.

I picture him, making and remaking these sheets, making and destroying, chasing a code (Image 21).

"The ultimate abstract expression in every art remains the number" (Kandinsky, quoted in Morganthaler, 1992[1921] p. 105).

You don't have to be a mathematician to have a feel for numbers. The relation to numbers is not necessarily scientific, and even when I was mentally disturbed, I had a lot of interest in numbers.

I got the idea that I would receive a message somehow. Later on I felt that I might get a divine revelation by seeing a certain number

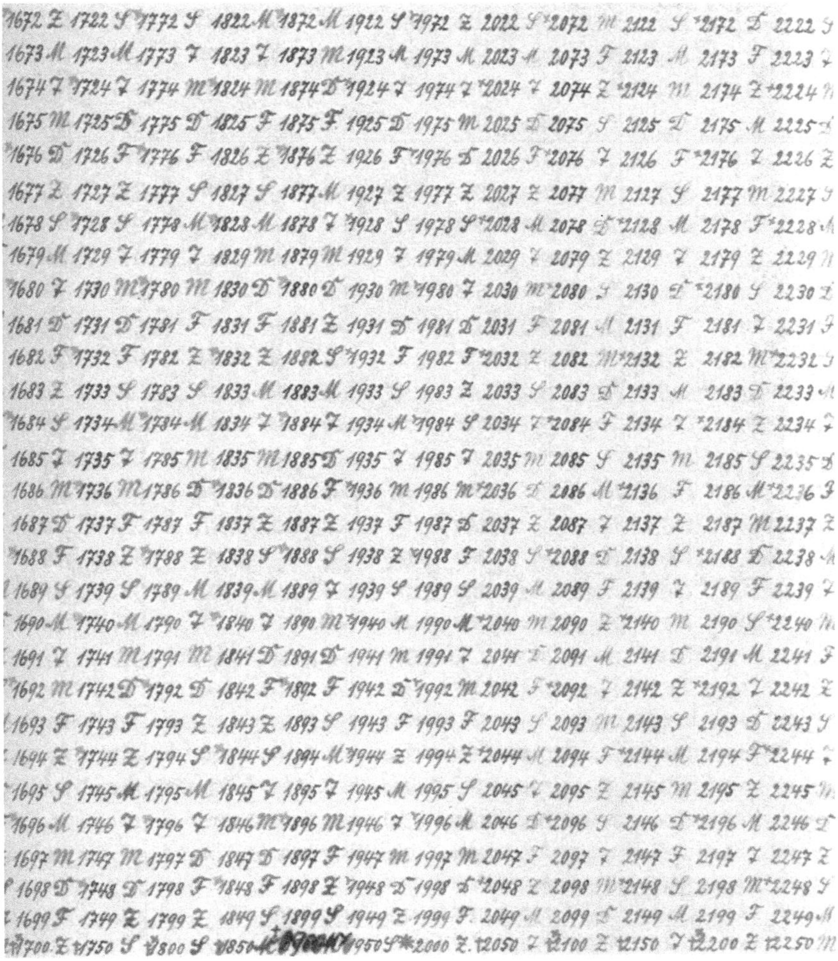

Image 21.   Joseph Heinrich Grebing, *Untitled*, undated, Inv. No. 624/6 recto.
          © Prinzhorn Collection, University Hospital Heidelberg.

that would appear. (John Nash, www.pbs.org/wgbh/amex/nash/
sfeature/sf_nash.html)

Image 22 shows pages from Grebing's *Notebook*.

As I look at Grebing's notebook, I think of a code unfolding without a key; it speaks of order, a scheme made of numbers, letters, and
little drawings. Joseph Grebing created handmade notebooks, filled

Image 22. Joseph Heinrich Grebing, *Notebook*, 1915–1921, Inv. No. 617.
© Prinzhorn Collection, University Hospital Heidelberg.

them with maps of the twentieth century, calendars, and snatches of his experiences. The drawings read as pictograms, and although the letters and numbers might refer to actual dates, I am not sure how to read them. I can make out "advent" but cannot translate most of the words. Is this idiosyncratic language, illegible language, or simply a German script I cannot read?

I sat at a desk in a room alone, working. The "celestial language" I was translating, I thought, would initiate a new time, because time was erasing humanity and destroying the universe. It was a coded alphabet, words combining to make new words, partly Latin, partly numerals, partly ideograms, and made of marks like those of the I-Ching, which worked as oracles. Always, time was of the essence. I was making an impossible translation of the voices that streamed through me, against short deadlines imposed by a deadly Other on the one hand, and against the wishes of the Catholic bishops, those who would burn me alive or poison me before the translation could be finished. I worked until I could not bear the tension, then I turned to homework, late into the night.

The dislocation of the translation, the imperfect art of making a distorted mark . . . Nur manchmal schiebt der / Vorhang der Pupille / sich laulos auf—On the sheet below you try, "Just now the pupil's noiseless shutter is lifted;" "only sometimes when the pupil's film is soundlessly lifted;" or you try, "yet at times, all noiseless, the pupil seems unveiled . . . At times the effort of translation seems to come too much to the front. (Kentridge, 2014, p. 153)

I worked to translate what streamed through me—voices speaking messages I could not decipher. Yet, I was obligated to record them and use them. The marks on the page spoke back to me differently, depending on whether they were arranged on a horizontal or vertical axis. On a vertical, they spoke omens of the future. On the horizontal, they read backwards, working as time machines to transport human-ity into the past. I was trying to make "celestial language": a code all humans could speak, all nations and peoples, for all time. I had no idea that a translation is a version, a betrayal of its original. I thought I was making a facsimile of what I was hearing, which, after all, made no sense. This translation was never finished. If anyone had asked how it worked as language, I could not have said. I worked on this language, if it can be called a language, from age sixteen until I was twenty-nine (Images 23a,b).

Writing involved "translation" of what I heard, but the translation was *given* to me, not invented by me. What I have shown here is a reconstruction; I no longer have access to what I wrote. The characters in my notebooks once spoke to me, an auditory experience of hearing and responding to language in ordered pieces, because I could not sustain a continuous flow of ideas.

In psychosis, perception of speech changes how one actually hears, as is evident in the following speech of a schizophrenic patient:

When people talk to me now it's like a different kind of language. It's too much to hold at once. My head is overloaded and I can't under-stand what they say. It makes you forget what you've heard because you can't get hearing it long enough. It's all in different bits which you have to put together again in your head – just words in the air. (Lawson et al., 1964, p. 375).

The attention of listeners is not drawn to the sounds of speech in them-selves but rather to the meanings conveyed by them and which they

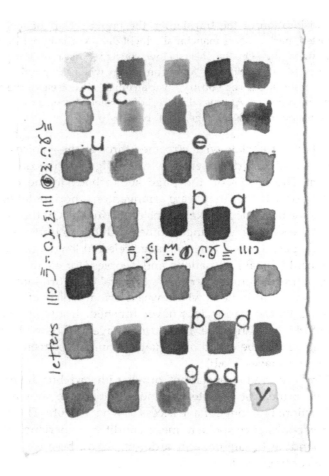

Image 23a.   Annie Rogers, *Celestial Alphabet,* watercolour, stamped letters and
pen on paper.

serve, in a sense, to deliver. It seems that, in listening to speech, our
awareness penetrates through the sound to reach a world of verbal
meaning beyond. And by the same token, that world is absolutely
silent—as silent, indeed, as are the pages of a book. In short, whereas
sound is the essence of music, language is mute. How do we come to
have this peculiar view of the silence of language, or, for that matter,
of the non-verbal nature of musical sound? (Ingold, 2007, p. 6)

In psychosis, it seems that language and music change places.
In the place of silently scanning words and sentences to find the

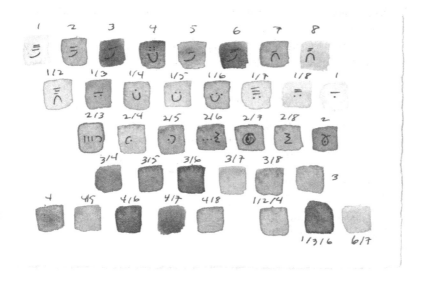

Image 23b.   Annie Rogers, *Celestial Alphabet,* watercolour, stamped letters and pen on paper.

meanings others also may hear and converse about, one is lost in language and sometimes cannot follow what is said. It is not possible to keep track of plausible meanings unfolding in a sentence. What then? Rather than listening to language as mute, language becomes musical, a series of sounds addressed to the listener and filled with significance. One searches in vain for a lost code that will scan, deliver meaning to language as enigma. To find such a code, one must create language, or notations, of another order. Here is Walter Morganthaler, a psychiatrist, writing about his patient, Adolph Wölfli:

> Our patient makes music by blowing into horns, which he makes out of thick paper bags . . . His musical notation takes two different forms: either he traces the lines of the staff (most often six) and fills them with the correct notes and bar lines, sharps, rests, clefs, and so on, or he writes out the notes with letters of the alphabet and indicates the meter by doubling the letters, underlining once or twice, crossing things out, and adding sharps and exclamation marks. Whether this alphabetical notation could be realized, I do not know. No one but the patient can read it correctly. (Morganthaler, 1992[1921], pp. 54–55)

Wölfli, a patient at the Waldau Clinic in Bern, Switzerland from 1885 to 1930, believed he was immortal, despite dying many times. Walter Morganthaler learnt that when Wölfli "died" he was always revived. He created a cosmology to depict where and how he would live after his death:

> In my own All-Powerful-Giant-Grand-Hall-of-St.-Adolf, all the gigantic crowds of gods, goddesses, and inhabitants of the most diverse and varied congregations, as soon as the festivities for my reception are completed, on numerous Transparent-Giant-Lightening-Butterflies, Birds and ditto, Snakes, to the other stars . . . (Morganthaler, 1992[1921], p. 48)

Images 24 and 25 are by Wölfli.

Wölfli creates a cosmology comprising spirals and musical notes in *Comet St. Adolph*, a wonderful juxtaposition of the endless time of circles and the specific time of music. In *The Poor Sinners' Stairway in St. Adolph-Summit*, Wölfli's numbers, writing, and repeating forms around the seven figures, which look uncannily alike, dominate the image. Wölfli's drawings fill the page, perhaps an aversion to empty spaces in his work. Morganthaler comments, "This *horror vacui* was already present in the first drawings we know" (Morganthaler, 1992[1921], p. 65).

Perhaps it is necessity to keep going, to fill the page, as a solution to words/thoughts/elements of speech that vanish suddenly, as if stolen or swept away by an outside force. Such moments erase all subjectivity, as if one is dead, a ghost, unable to think, speak, act, or breach a void in meaning in any way. Whatever code Wölfli is working out, it is full, repetitive, and commands his days for decades. His art encompasses letters and words, musical notation and numbers. It has no gaps, no blanks, and yet he cannot explain how it works, and neither does he claim this art as a subject of his own experience. Morganthaler remarks that it is not uncommon to hear him assert that it is not he himself who invents all his pictures. Instead, he has drawn by divine order during his trips through the universe. Wölfli exclaims, "Do you really think I could just make this all up in my head?" (Morganthaler, 1992[1921], pp. 23–24).

The psychotic subject, however, might succeed in establishing a new subjective position by adopting speech elements or autonyms that have been imposed, using them to identify a meaningful task, mission, or purpose. In this way, building delusion not only works to

Image 24.   Adolf Wölfli, *Komeet Skt.Adolf/Comet St. Adolph*, 1916, pencil and
coloured pencil on paper, 53.0 x 42.7 cm.
© Adolf Wölfli Foundation, Museum of Fine Arts Bern, Switzerland.

stabilise the experience of psychosis, but also to create a new position
for the subject.

   This subjective position could include making new language, what
I call *incandescent alphabets*, but the language will be idiosyncratic, and

Image 25. Adolf Wölfli (1864–1930). *Die Armsünder=Treppe in Skt.Adolf=Höhn/
The Poor Sinners' Stairway in St. Adolf-Summit*, 1914. Geographic and
Algebraic Books, Book 12, p. 217. Pencil and coloured pencil on
paper, 99.6/100.1 x 71.8/72.2 cm.
© Adolf Wölfli Foundation, Museum of Fine Arts Bern, Switzerland.

the code to understand it, or to make it work, will not function as a system of language (with multiple meanings, nuances, and possible interpretations shared by others) so much as a code. As a combinatory new system, the elements must always mean *one thing*, if combined or calculated correctly. The elements and their combinations are not open to question or to interpretation *outside of the code itself*. The code reinstates the logic of the autonyms—it is complete, even as it emerges, and cannot be questioned.

August Klett created such an alphabet and language. He had been a wine and champagne merchant, but became increasingly eccentric, withdrew to his bed, and lacerated his abdomen with a knife. Inside the Heidelberg Asylum, he was lost to his hallucinations. Then he began to draw and write. He created a "colour alphabet" of letters and numbers in 1905 that he sent to his uncle for use in his dyeing business. Here is a tiny part of the alphabet: "1A = England = red, red beets; 4d = sunlight yellow = road dust coloured; 14 o = white as day, Austria-Hungary; 20 u = Green = frog = Russia . . ." (Prinzhorn, 1972[1922], p. 133) (Image 26).

I have taken the liberty of turning this image on its side so that we can see what dominates the face is the order inscribed into the profile,

Image 26.   August Klett (Pseudonym Klotz), *Worm Holes*, 1919, Inv. No. 568.
© Prinzhorn Collection, University Hospital Heidelberg.

repeating worms with human heads, and human heads inside the rounded shapes of worm holes. As though the drawing were not enough, Klett created a language in which words were combined to make new words, elements devoid of meaning except, perhaps, that they spoke to Klett himself. The words form a code: an order constructed through dashes, parentheses, word combinations, a few numbers, and equal signs: "Worm holes (bath faces) worm paths (pianomusicstickteeth) worm strong (spitbathlife of the archlyregallery-tintimlier-reflections: ad mothersugarmoon in the sevensaltnosewater . . ." (Prinzhorn, 1972[1922], p. 142).

Klett's art and writing might well serve as an elaborate code for an experience that continued to be imposed on him. Is this work, as Prinzhorn suggests, "an endless, aimless, somehow enjoyable game" (p. 143), or is it a serious effort to reinstate order and a subjective position within that order? I do not know, but I think it is possible that Klett was making a code as a life work; and perhaps that code gave him a place and a purpose after hallucinations had taken from him his place in the world, and his purpose among others.

What of the illegible writing of psychotics? Is this work a language that can be read, an open, uncodified script, or it does it mean something very particular to the writer that others cannot read or discern? Whatever it is, whether illegible, or barely legible, or privately legible, writing scribbles and scripts around and within drawings seems to be one of the signatures of psychotic art. I wonder if these artists were actively experimenting with the unknown, that edge of the unreadable in language? Currently, writers and artists use the term "asemic writing" to refer to experimental writing that has no semantic content (Jacobson & Gaze, 2013). Josiah McElheny (2013) summarises the forms adopted by Emily Dickinson (using pieces of envelops to shape her poetry) and by Robert Walser (who wrote in tiny script in pencil on found scraps):

> Ephemeral works on paper that are gorgeous and mysterious, they are hybrid forms that speak about the situational specificity of language and the tension between word as representation and word as specific object . . . they also contain drafts of texts that are fantastic in any format. (McElheny, 2013, p. 51)

I cannot think of a better way to describe the work of the next three artists–writers.

Writing: scripts and scribbles

I know very little of these three artists–writers. The first is Barbara Suckfüll (Image 27), who was a farmer's wife living at the Werneck Asylum following her diagnosis of dementia praecox (schizophrenia).

The next, Emma Bachmayer, lived in the Regensburg Asylum with the same diagnosis. I only know that she was Catholic and single (Image 28).

Then there is Heinrich Mebes, who was a Protestant watchmaker, again diagnosed with dementia praecox (schizophrenia) (Image 29). I chose these three examples among many forms of writing in the Prinzhorn Collection to capture a range of forms: scribbles, as well as art comprising scripts and art created alongside scripts.

Barbara Suckfüll wrote printed words in addition to works that combined drawing and writing:

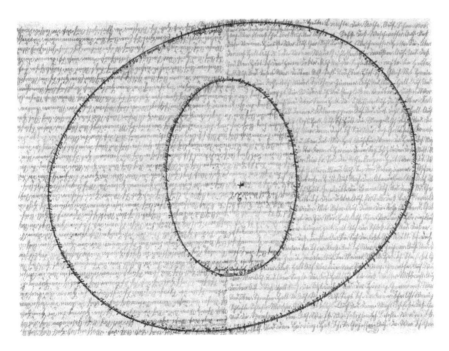

Image 27. Barbara Suckfüll, Untitled, 1910, Inv. No. 1956 verso.
© Prinzhorn Collection, University Hospital Heidelberg.

Image 28.   Emma Bachmeyer, *Untitled*, 1912, Inv. 4730.
© Prinzhorn Collection, University Hospital Heidelberg.

And. Today. Is. Sunday. Too. The. First. Sunday. After. The.
Assumption. Too. And. So. It. Will. Be. The. Twenty-first. This. Is. Fine.
I. Think. And. That. Is. The. Washbasin. You. See. I. Have. Drawn.
That. Too. One. Time. Too. And. Then. Today. The. Redhead. Brought.
Cold. Washing. Water. It. Was. Too. Cold. What. She. Brought. Today.
And. The. Second. Devil. Was. On. The. Lookout. I. Heard. That.
Myself. Too. (Clausen et al., 1996, p. 175)

This passage is wonderfully lucid, down to the day of the week
and the cold washing water. Even the devil seems quite ordinary here.
While Suckfüll's art looks like an ornate "O" over tiny, almost illegible, lighter script that is not easy to decipher, her printed text is legible and readable, every word punctuated, made to stand still for a
moment.

Heinrich Mebes writes a script within his egg-shape, and though I
cannot read it, it reads as writing.

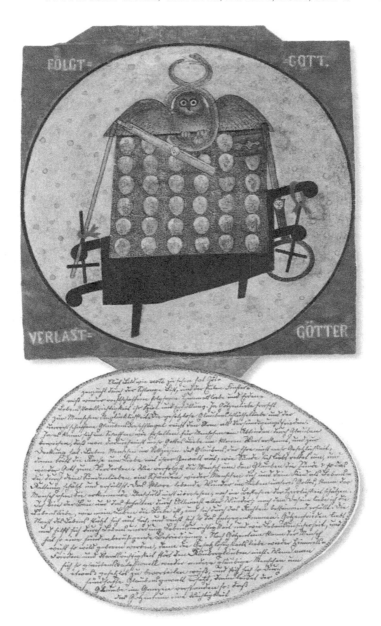

Image 29.   Heinrich Hermann Mebes, *Follow God Abandon Gods*, undated,
Inv. 413 recto.
© Prinzhorn Collection, University Hospital Heidelberg.

Emma Backmayer's pen on paper appears as scribbles, but who is to say that it is, or is not, writing?

What is writing? What, of this writing, is imagined by the artist as written and, therefore, composed? Is there some requirement that it be something legible *to us*, reading it a century or more later, in another language?

At my little round table in my office, I use a magnifying glass to look closely at the intricate lines of this writing. I do not know if it is meant to speak or not; it is singularly marvellous and inventive.

As I look at the art, writing, scripts, scribbles, all made by psychotics of the last century, I wonder what, if anything, is metaphoric about it? A metaphor, when it works, forms a bridge to other meanings, after all. Poetry works by extending new horizons of meaning in relation to a metaphor. Yet, this art of calendars, clocks, numbers, repeating forms, combined words, writing of scripts and scribbles, does not seem to connect with *any* collective meaning.

I wonder if these systems of order, however, connect particular floating autonyms in the psychotic's experience in a way that nothing else will serve, and this art creates new meanings she or he might then grasp.

In his book, *The Subject of Psychosis: A Lacaninan Perspective* (2011) Stijn Vanheule considers the possibility that the psychotic constructs an "axiom" (p. 116) of delusion, a key idea that explains his experience. This explanation places him utterly at the disposal of a perverse Other. In the face of this terrible predicament, the subject introduces an *opposing* signifier, a protestation against the "signifier of the Other's madness" (p. 117). Finally, the subject takes up a work, mission, or project that is a compromise between what the mad Other demands and his own protest. The new work is *itself* a new subjective position. Vanheule describes how this happens:

> As a delusion is elaborated, a change in the condition of autonymous speech elements can be observed. Whereas at first they are experienced as "intimate exteriorities," as communications from without that touch on the intimacy of a person's being, their status changes to that of what I call "exterior intimacies," in that they gradually start to be the intimate poles around which discourse is organized. (p. 110)

Such a position implies an active construction that transforms the psychotic's language in order to oppose the signifiers of a mad Other, and to reconfigure them in a new way.

Hyacinth Freiherr von Wieser (pseudonym Heinrich Welz), another artist of the Prinzhorn Collection, drew many geometric forms (Image 30). Prinzhorn (1972[1922]), looking at the development of this art over time, asks, "What element in the drawing gives us the feeling of regularity, while we think of arbitrariness without arriving at a balance?" (p. 199). He concludes that, despite the fact that von Wieser persists with impossible ideas, in his art "regularity and arbitrariness are finally combined and developed, if you will, into a valid, formal language" (p. 199).

Commenting on this drawing, Prinzhorn explains, "Welz [von Wieser] assumes various centers from which lines of force radiate, in keeping with projections of thoughts and the polarization of the human body in relation to the earth and other bodies" (Prinzhorn, 1972[1922], pp. 198–199). Von Wieser developed a new relation to the

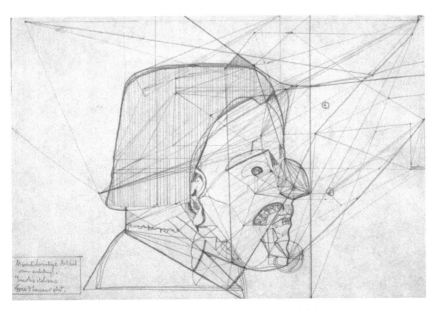

Image 30.   Hyacinth Freiherr von Wieser (pseudonym Welz),
              Geometrical portrait "Männlichwürdige Art hat man unbedingt",
              undated, Inv. No. 2458 recto.
              © Prinzhorn Collection, University Hospital Heidelberg.

polarities that controlled him; he could spin around rapidly and over-come the attraction of the earth, and believed he could actually ascend (Image 31). Perhaps this was a gesture that signified his opposition to the lines of force imposed on him.

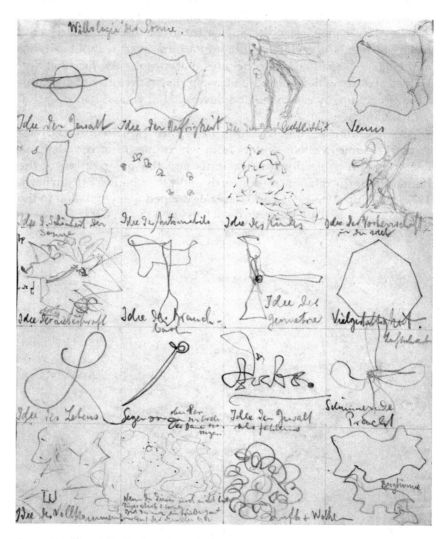

Image 31.   Hyacinth Freiherr von Wieser (pseudonym Welz), *Willology of the Sun,* Inv. No. 2440.
© Prinzhorn Collection, University Hospital Heidelberg.

Willology of the Sun reads as a chart of how the cosmos works. It is composed of both scribbles and scripts, accompanied by drawn figures. Prinzhorn comments that his patient "believes that whatever fills his mind completely finds expression in graphic representation" (Prinzhorn, 1972[1922], p. 199) (Image 32).

This is one of the last drawings that von Wieser produced. The major centres of Napoleon's campaigns map on to this beautiful curve, and the lines that connect those places form a capital "N". According to Prinzhorn, von Wieser said that if we trace the curve several times daily with our heads, we will be able to understand Napoleon's thoughts and acts.

It seems that this very idea, spoken to Prinzhorn, connects von Wieser in his delusion with a collective; we, too, can experience Napoleon's perspective, quite literally.

But, of course, we cannot do this.

In the end, von Wieser stopped drawing and speaking. He said that he would "simply strew graphite over his drawing paper and would force the particles into lines and forms by staring at them" (p. 200).

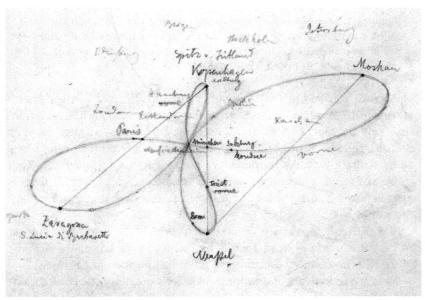

Image 32. Hyacinth Freiherr von Wieser (pseudonym Welz), *Napoleon's Curve*, Inv. No. 2439.
© Prinzhorn Collection, University Hospital Heidelberg.

Following Vanheule, I wonder if von Wieser created, in opposition to a delusional axiom concerning a universe of controlling polarities, a language of curves and gestures. If this is the case, his work solved an enigma that language cannot really solve; the drawn curve could make another's (Napoleon's) thought fully accessible across time and space. The magic of drawing applied to thoughts. Von Wieser reduced his wonderful geometries to the idea that *thinking of drawing* would create a finished drawing. There was no need to draw in time and space any longer. Has he wrestled back his agency, his subjectivity, with this coded language of drawing curves and lines propelled by his own magical thoughts? He believed that he could (and we can) relive history in a curve.

Again, I come to the problem of Time. What is Time, and to what extent can we play with it?

> In the studio I film my eight-year-old son. He takes a jar of paint and a handful of pencils, some books and papers. He throws the jar of paint across the studio walls, scatters the pencils, tears the papers and scatters the shards. We run the film in reverse. There is a utopian perfection. The papers reconstruct themselves every time. He gathers them all. He catches twelve pencils, all arriving from different corners of the room in the same moment. In the jar he catches all the paint— not a drop is spilled. The wall is pristine. His joy at his own skill is overflowing. "Can I do it again?" (Kentridge, 2014, p. 106)

William Kentridge with his son in the studio; we can see them, making a film in reverse. First, we can imagine the boy and his elation. Time can be rearranged. Sequence can be reversed, and, as it is reversed, relived. More accurately, reversed, it is lived for *the first time* in this strange way. As humans, we are fascinated with time, how it can be arranged, rearranged, written, rewritten. To play with time is not psychotic. But the sheer necessity to find a new way to represent time might be.

It is difficult to convey the extent to which the psychotic subject can be left outside of time. Just as he cannot make language work as it once did, he cannot comprehend what has happened to time.

As I turn to look at contemporary versions of an infinite code (calendars, ratios, drawing with repeating forms) made by psychotic artists, again it is not easy to find or identify this art. I am filled with joy when I see it in *Raw Vision* (Winter 2012–2013), a journal dedicated to artists named as outsider, brut, folk, naïve, intuitive, and visionary. In an article by Tony Thorne, "Heavenly city—John Devlin's utopian visions" (pp. 42–45), I discover art that arrests me, takes my breath away, because it is so like the art of his historical predecessors. Devlin, I learn, had an experience of epiphany and a mental breakdown when he was a Divinity student at Edmund's College, Cambridge University in 1979. He returned to Nova Scotia in Canada, resided in a hospital for a time, and then lived at home. He volunteers with the Nova Scotia Art Gallery, struggles with the side effects of his medication, and creates art.

Devlin has created a utopian world called Nova Cantabrigiensis, an imaginary city, an artificial island on the North Atlantic coast of Canada. His art includes drawings, annotations, dates, formulae, diagrams, symbols, and repeating forms. These works are made of layers of paper, glued together. On the verso are numerical sequences developed according to mystical principles. He explains to Tony Thorne (2012–2013):

> My theory is that for ideal design, there is an Ideal Ratio. I have been hunting for such a constant. I was on a Faustian Quest for arcane knowledge that would explain the magical ambience of Cambridge. I thought that if I could capture that ambience as a mathematical formula, then I wouldn't have to go to England. I thought I could think my way out of mental illness, back to the happy times in Cambridge before things began to fall apart on me. (pp. 43–44)

> Images 33 and 34 are examples of Devlin's work.

> It is possibly of minor interest that the dimensions of the Canadian dollar bill match the ratio of the major architectural elements of two Cambridge University collegiate monuments. The crisis of the euro would be over if they adopted 11:24 as the ratio for their paper currency . . . no wonder there is a euro banking crisis: and the solution is so simple. (Thorne, 2012, p. 45)

Image 35 is also by John Devlin.

Again, I encounter marvellous geometries and magical thinking, this time in opposition to mental illness, with the promise of a restoration of another time, and a solution to world problems.

Utopia: time stops, before disorder. The time created is a new time, a new alphabet for how to measure, consider, and live in that time.

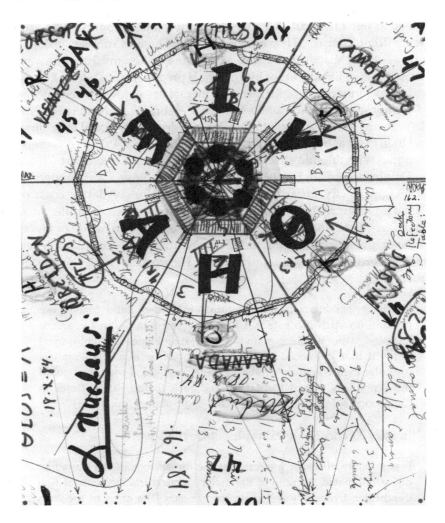

Image 33. John Devlin, *Untitled no. 162*, 21 April 1988, mixed media on paper, 27.94 x 21.59 cm.
Courtesy of John Devlin and Gallery Christian Berst Art Brut.

I am interested to see that Devlin moves among detailed drawings of place, to repeating forms, to schematic diagrams. As an artist, he simplifies; he turns to numbers; he seeks a ratio.

I read Devlin's art as a search for a code to make sense of an epiphany that was, and perhaps remains, enigmatic, unreadable, an experience that he summons and constructs in his art.

Image 34. John Devlin, *Untitled no. 120*, 11 January 1989, mixed media on paper, 27.94 x 21.59 cm.
Courtesy of Henry Boxer Gallery, London.

I look at his art and revel in its beauty, the magic of its incandescent alphabets and numbers, created as if to signify a new subjective position, a new time, and a corrective ratio. His art speaks to me in ways I cannot begin to convey with words.

*   *   *

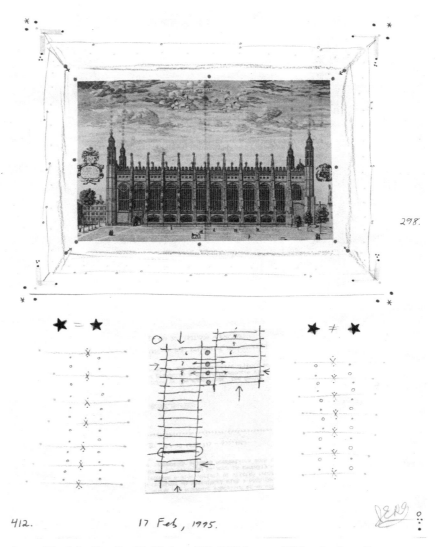

Image 35. John Devlin, *Untitled no. 298*, 17 February 1995, mixed media on
paper, 27.94 x 21.59 cm. Courtesy of Henry Boxer Gallery, London.

I return to the Lavender Door, walking though a dusting of fresh snow
from my office at Austen Riggs. There, I find Mark Mulherrin waiting
for me inside the painting studio. It is cold and I shed layers: coat,
scarf, hat. I sit on a high stool and we talk. I show him the images of

this chapter, especially the scripts, because I am curious about how he will read them.

Mark asks me if I have ever seen the film *Crumb*, directed by Terry Zwigoff. At my blank look he asks if I know of Robert Crumb. "Famous cartoonist?" Mark prompts. No. Mark tells me the film is primarily about Robert, but his family, including his brother Charles, make an appearance. Charles was mentally ill and lived as a recluse at home with his mother. Mark sees a parallel between the art of psychotics that we both find compelling and the work of Charles Crumb. Mark explains, "Charles also made cartoons, and he moved from cartooning to distorted figures to speech bubbles, the text taking over, to just writing, to scribbles—tiny gestures that look like writing but can't be read." Is this the evolution of change in language for him, we wonder, or is it a trace of getting more and more lost? We do not know. After the film was made, in February, 1993, Charles committed suicide.

Mark sits and "writes" scripts—letter-like forms that are not letters. He made them as a child, and muttered to himself as he wrote, as if speaking the writing. What is this? It is so familiar to me, and yet distinctive, *his* way of writing. What is writing, after all, if not first and foremost, a form of thinking, thinking the unthinkable for ourselves?

> I find and repeat the list four or five times in different notebooks . . .
> Each time I expect the list to be different; each time to my surprise, it
> is the same, or almost the same. But in the reordering, the slight shift,
> the word that is illegible, we make some new crack, a new element
> enters the list, makes a space for itself—and this is the guest we have
> been waiting for. (Kentridge, 2014, p. 117)

Donald Mitchell, an African-American artist diagnosed as schizophrenic with mild mental retardation (Rivers, 2004), makes art that seems to me a visual representation of what Kentridge describes: figures repeat, almost the same, but not the same, as if each one is a new crack, a new element, "the guest we have been waiting for". Mitchell's figures are uncannily alike with their big heads and smaller squared torsos.

On the page, his figures repeat and become superimposed; they emerge from, and recede into, his wonderful cross-hatched spaces, proliferate and dissolve, repeating in the signature of true outsider art: a new visual alphabet (Image 36).

The art of this chapter, made by those who have entered madness, those have exited, and those who have not, carries a signature of their constructed, lived experience: figures repeat, merge with writing; writing turns into scripts and scribbles, writing with and without letters, writing that dissolves. I read them all as incandescent alphabets, speaking a code that is missing from language, making a form for experiences that are otherwise unpresentable. Whatever it means or once meant to the makers, they are artists–writers making something utterly original with words and images (Image 37).

I imagine Grebing making this object for his writing with the materials he could assemble in an asylum. It contains folded spaces for inserts; layered, cut, and assembled, it is an object any writer might envy. It is, *itself*, a work of marvellous visual complexity and yearning.

Image 36.   Donald Mitchell, *Untitled* (superimposed figures), 1996, ink on paper, 18 x 24.5 in. Image courtesy of Creative Growth Art Center.

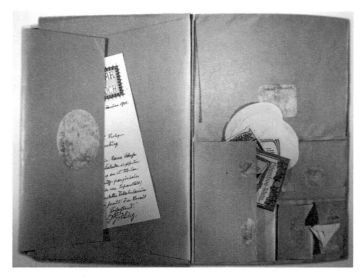

Image 37.   Joseph Heinrich Grebing, *Writing Materials*, undated, Inv. No. 612.
© Prinzhorn Collection, University Hospital Heidelberg.

CHAPTER FIVE

After the disaster: six sketches and a short play

I n his book, *The Writing of the Disaster* (1995[1980]), Maurice Blanchot defines disaster in the following way: "The disaster . . . is what escapes the very possibility of experience—it is the limit of writing. This must be repeated: the disaster de-scribes" (p. 7).

The disaster registers but escapes "the very possibility of experience", and, at the limit of writing, acts to dissolve meaning, to undo writing. Ann Smock, the translator for *The Writing of the Disaster* (1995[1980]), comments on reading Blanchot in her translator's remarks,

> Blanchot lets thoughts suggest themselves and develop through puns, alliterations, rhymes, etymologies (both learned and fanciful), as though thought were engraved in words themselves and thinking consisted in deciphering the inscription, or as if language were speaking to us in the various sonorities of diverse terms, and we had only to listen to what it tells . . . (p. vii)

After the disaster of psychosis, a mental breakdown that breaks down speech and writing, how do writers find a way with words— "listening to what it tells" and making language do what it used to do, and more? The "more" I refer to here restores language, renews language for humanity. The writers in this chapter each treat language as a new object; their words carry effects that speak beyond the individuals, in the wake of the same kind of disaster that Blanchot invokes, which is, after all, human existence at the edge of a great void, and a part of being human. The disaster puts our own experience, our very existence, out of reach; all meanings or interpretations are erased.

This space in which meanings are erased is what Lacan in his later work called the unconscious. "When the l'esp of a laps, that is since I can only write in French: when the space of a lapsus no longer carries any meaning (or interpretation), only then is one sure that one is in the unconscious. One *knows*" (Lacan, 1981[1977], *Seminar XI*, p. vii). A lapsus is a blunder, a moment that interrupts an emergent intended direction or meaning in speech. Like the space in which the psychotic finds no word, no thought to signify existence, the moment of a lapsus usurps what the subject wants to say and leaves her in the lurch with respect to meaning. The lapsus is the disaster that de-scribes, erases meaning.

For Colette Soler, a Lacanian analyst, the space of a lapsus is the territory of the real unconscious. In her book, *Lacan: The Unconscious Reinvented* (2014), she writes,

> The real unconscious is neological, if neologism consists in giving to words the weight of an ineffable and personal jouissance. Made of signifiers outside the chain and implanted in the field of jouissance— that the lapsus shows without deciphering—it is the *psychotic kernel of every speaking being*. (pp. 44–45, my italics)

Let us pause here, before speaking in language for every speaking being. Perhaps you have stood at a doorway and listened to the speech of a baby as she approximates words in a stream of sounds and inflections. Speech is melody, song, before it is language. Each of us retains this possibility to speak and to write "giving to words the weight of an ineffable and personal jouissance". Here, I am referring to what Lacan called "the third jouissance". In a paper he presented in Rome in 1974 (Lacan, 2006), Lacan spoke of the third *jouissance* as *jouis-sens*, the *jouissance* of meaning, the *jouissance* of the unconscious. What is this *jouissance*, this "psychotic kernel" of ineffable, intimate musicality? John Muller called this music in the voice "sonority" (Muller, 2014, p. 54). It is at the heart of our humanity, our capacity to hear words as music, and our bodily response to human voices before voices spoke meanings.

What is at play in writing, both inside and outside psychosis, is something melodious in language, music put to use to say something, and yet to sing without signification. Lacan (1989) called it "lalangue". To explain this marvellous word play would be, in effect, to kill it in transmission, so I am going to present a short play. The characters are six writers, all but the first one of them acknowledged as writers of reputation: Barbara Suckfüll, Robert Walser, Janet Frame, James Joyce, Emily Dickinson, and Tomas Tranströmer.

Two of the writers (Janet Frame and Emily Dickinson, and their biographers, on the whole) refuse any possibility or reference to psychosis, even mental illness. Although Lacan gave a whole seminar premised on Joyce having a psychotic structure, James Joyce never experienced a psychotic crisis. Tomas Tranströmer was never hospitalised during his single, adolescent experience with a crisis, or later in his life for mental illness of any kind. This would leave me with Barbara Suckfüll and Robert Walser only. Why include the other writers, then? I am interested in psychosis as a structure, not limited to madness as an outcome. I chose these six writers because they each speak to the experience of a conundrum with language, not once, here or there, but eloquently, repeatedly, upholding humanity (inside, outside, or despite mental illness). They push the limits of language, making language work as music, making language into incandescent alphabets.

Let me introduce the writers. Even if you know them already, here they are characters with parts to play. People have written volumes about them; I have decided to sketch their lives, including a few references that are crucial to the play itself, and give my reason for choosing each one.

Barbara Suckfüll was a farmer when she began to hear voices at age fifty. In 1910, as a resident of the Heidelberg Asylum, while listening to voices, she began to draw–write word-pictures. She drew what was there: cutlery, her washbasin. She marked the entire page with images and words, and used a pin to make tiny holes in her compositions. She often turned the page around to work the other side. She punctuated each word with a stopping point, writing in a way that, literally, arrested language.

Stuart Brisley made a video, *About Barbara Suckfüll*, performed in 2010. He presented her words in Polish and English, in both female and male voices. He added sounds, a sound tape running through the performance in a slow rhythm; the sound of rain, some ambulance sounds, and amplified sounds of tin cans and a broom sweeping, as well as "wooden chair sounds being dragged across the marble floor, a groaning screaming harsh scratching, a parallel expression to her written text" (Brisley, 2014).

Barbara Suckfüll was able to leave the asylum. In a report about a home visit with her after her discharge, the doctor noted in 1934 that she was mentally well. I translated this delightful fact from the German on the Prinzhorn Collection website (prinzhorn.ukl-hd.de).

I chose Suckfüll for my play because she writes in the tempo of one word at a time, speaking to her immediate surroundings and impressions. Her voice stands out among the others in its repetition, its insistence on what is there.

The Swiss writer Robert Walser published nine novels, among them, *The Tanner Children* (1906), *Jakob von Gunten* (1909), and *The Robber* (1925) before he was hospitalised. Walser experimented with writing in pencil. He was diagnosed with schizophrenia and confined in the Bernese Mental Institution in Waldau, where he continued to write, using only his pencil and a radically miniaturised version of a script called *Kurrent*, a form of handwriting in German-speaking countries taught in schools up until the 1940s. Medieval in its origins, all up-and-down slanting angles, an *e* is represented by a simple pair of vertical ticks like a quotation mark, an *s* by a mere slash. In ordinary size writing the script is difficult, but not impossible, to read. Walser wrote in pencil, and his characters were only one millimetre high. He wrote on ephemera, small scraps of paper that came his way, pieces of newspaper, backs of envelopes. This writing was finally translated and introduced to English speaking readers by Susan Bernofsky in the 2010 publication of Walser's *The Microscripts*.

Walser moved to the Herisau Sanatorium in 1933, where he died of a heart attack on a walk in the snow in 1956. Billy Childs, a British artist, made a painting of Walser lying on his back, dead in the snow.

In her review of *The Microscripts*, "From the pencil zone: Robert Walser's masterworklets", Rivka Galchen captures something of Walser's relation to writing:

The words start to write themselves, *trove* to *trovato*, like some auto-matic-writing experiment gone horribly right. Here language is not a barrier to the perfect expression of self; instead, language is bliss *because* it is its own thing, determining its own course, running roughshod over the speaker. . . . Walser sounds not so much like he's creating but rather like he's taking dictation, working as a kind of copy clerk, but for whom? An air of the holy fool pervades. And the final irony is how singular the voice of all this self-effacement is. (*Harpers*, 2010, pp. 78)

I made a small artist book in honour of Walser, layering images of his writing from *The Microscripts* with my own tiny pencil writings. I chose Walser because each sentence speaks something stunning about those moments that most of us simply overlook as insignificant.

Janet Frame was born into a working class family living in poverty in Dunedin, New Zealand in 1924. Her brother had epilepsy, and Janet lost two sisters to drowning. As a child, Frame and her sisters lived in world of imaginary games and literary efforts. Early in her life, Frame wanted to be a poet. However, she became a trainee teacher as a young adult, and suffered a mental breakdown. She spent the greater part of a decade in mental hospitals, with a diagnosis of schizophre-nia. When her first book, *The Lagoon and Other Stories* (1951) won a prestigious literary prize, her doctors at Seacliff Hospital decided not to carry out a planned leucotomy. She was discharged from the hospi-tal in 1955. The writer Frank Sargeson took her in and supported her, creating the conditions that allowed her to write her first novel, *Owls Do Cry* (1982a[1960]), a novel that depicts stunning parallels to Frame's life; an epileptic boy, the death of a sibling, and an experience in a brutal mental asylum. Frame eventually moved to London, where she twice went into the Maudsley Hospital. There, her doctors declared she was not, and had never been, schizophrenic. She was shy all her life and insistently reclusive, going so far as to live under a pseudonym: Janet Clutha. From 1964 to the end of her life, Frame lived in New Zealand as a writer, where she died in 2004 (King, 2004).

Frame wrote twelve novels, including one published after her death, *Towards Another Summer* (2007). She was New Zealand's premier writer; no one can doubt her originality and genius. She wrote an autobiography in three volumes (Volume One: *To the Is-Land* (1982b); Volume Two: *An Angel at My Table* (1984a); Volume Three: *The Envoy from Mirror City* (1984b). Jane Campion created a film based on these works: *An Angel at my Table* in 1990. The film called attention to Frame's writing, which led to a worldwide reputation, albeit linked to her mental illness. Michael King (2001) wrote a biography: *Wrestling with the Angel: A Life of Janet Frame*, a work that agrees she was not schizophrenic, but also undermines her genius.

It does not matter much to me whether or not Frame was "schizophrenic". I chose her because she writes *At the Edge of the Alphabet* (1962), the title of one of her novels. She makes the alphabet shine as she evokes states of bewilderment and mental collapse among her characters, and she evokes the unforgettable desolation of a psychiatric ward.

James Joyce born on 2 February 1882, in Rathgar, a Dublin suburb. Joyce left Ireland in 1902 to pursue a medical education in Paris, and did not return until the following year when his mother was dying. He drifted in and out of medical school in Paris before taking up residence in Zurich. In 1905, he completed a collection of stories, *Dubliners*, though it was not until 1913 that the volume was actually printed. During these frustrating and impoverished years, Joyce relied upon the emotional support of his lover, Nora Barnacle, as well as the financial support of his younger brother, Stanislaus Joyce. Both Nora and Stanislaus remained supporting figures for the duration of the writer's life. During the eight years between *Dubliners'* completion and publication, Joyce and Barnacle had two children, a son, Giorgio, and a daughter, Lucia. Ezra Pound was key to serialising *A Portrait of the Artist as a Young Man* in 1914 and 1915. The book was printed in New York in 1916, and in London in 1917. Joyce came into contact with Harriet Shaw Weaver, who served as both editor and patron while Joyce wrote *Ulysses*. *Ulysses* was published in Paris in 1922. Joyce endured eleven eye operations to salvage his ever-worsening eyesight, beginning mid-way through writing *Ulysses*. The novel was banned in Britain and the USA on obscenity charges. In 1934, Random House won a court battle to print *Ulysses* in the USA; two years later, the novel was legalised in Britain. By that time, Joyce had concluded his seventeen-year "work in progress", *Finnegans Wake*. Even more baffling and convoluted than *Ulysses*, *Finnegans Wake* was a critical failure. On 13 January 1941, Joyce died of a stomach ulcer at the age of fifty-eight, and was buried in Zurich (Ellman, 1983[1959]).

Impossible not to include Joyce among my writers! I have read him since adolescence, walked Dublin in his footsteps, taught him, annotated him, puzzled over him, read him again (alongside Lacan), and witnessed a former student, Derek Pyle, create a musical version of the unabridged *Finnegans Wake* (www.waywordsandmeansigns. com). I chose Joyce because he has taken the English language apart and created a new language.

Emily Dickinson was born in 1830, in Amherst, Massachusetts. She attended Mount Holyoke Female Seminary in South Hadley, but only for one year. Throughout her life, she seldom left her home but she wrote many letters and read widely. Her brother, Austin, who attended law school and became an attorney, lived next door with his wife, Susan Gilbert. Dickinson never walked the short distance to their home. Dickinson, a recluse in the town, was unwilling to be seen by visitors even within the household; she became a voice, dressed in white, listening at the threshold of her bedroom door. In his study of the Dickinson family, psychiatrist John Cody (1971) concluded that Dickinson was psychotic, experiencing a complete mental breakdown during the crisis years of 1861–1863, but almost all her biographers disagree, softening and omitting any oddity or anguish in her life.

Whatever we do or do not know of her mental life, Dickinson was extremely prolific as a poet and regularly enclosed poems in letters to friends. She died in Amherst in 1886. After her death, her family discovered forty hand-bound volumes of nearly 1,800 poems, or "fascicles", in her bedroom. Dickinson had assembled these booklets by folding and sewing five or six sheets of stationery paper and copying what seem to be final versions of poems. The handwritten poems show a variety of dash-like marks of various sizes and directions (some are even vertical). The editor of her complete poems, Thomas H. Johnson (1961) removed her unusual and varied dashes, replacing them with traditional punctuation. The original order of the poems was restored when Ralph W. Franklin used the physical evidence of the paper itself to re-create her intended order, relying on smudge marks, needle punctures, and other clues to reassemble the packets he published as *The Manuscript Books of Emily Dickinson* (1981).

Dickinson also composed in pencil on scraps, mostly envelopes, many cut or torn into shapes for her writing. The poems on these odd scraps of paper are utterly singular in grammar, form, and sensibility. She turned the edges to write sometimes, a process documented in *The Gorgeous Nothings*, compiled and presented by Jen Bervin and Marta Werner in 2013. Perhaps more than any other poet, Dickinson's poems lose something of their essence when transferred into the conventions of print.

I have read Dickinson since adolescence, and have lived in her town for twelve years now. I was invited recently (as a poet, along with other local poets) to sit alone for an hour in her bedroom and write. In a room stripped bare of wallpaper, even the mantelpiece dismantled (it was being restored at the time), I wrote ". . . this room makes / a satisfying / little orbit / hinged here / with flickering lines" (Rogers, 2015, p. 32).

I chose Dickinson because I believe she *was* shattered, and from that shattering she became a poet and wrote glittering short lines in a halting cadence littered with dashes.

In April 1931, Tomas Tranströmer was born in Stockholm, Sweden. His mother, who divorced his father when he was an infant, raised her son alone. He experienced a crisis during his adolescence that he wrote about in an autobiography, *Memoirs Look at Me* (1995). What happened to him after his crisis of dread that he could speak to no one in adolescence? He attended the University of Stockholm, where he studied psychology and poetry. Tranströmer became a psychologist, working with juvenile delinquents in his native Sweden. He also became a poet, producing and publishing stunning poems, beginning in his early twenties. Tranströmer sold thousands of volumes in his native country, and his work has been translated into more than fifty languages. His books of poetry translated into English have reached a wide readership. Following a stroke in 1990 that took away the use of his right hand and all but short phrases of speech, his wife, Monica, began speaking for him in the world. He published a short memoir and two books of poetry after his stroke.

In 2011, he won the Nobel Prize in Literature. The world of poetry, which had awaited this award on his behalf for decades, applauded. In a short film by Pamela Robertson-Pierce and Neil Astley about the moment the news broke, we see a crowd of journalists in the stairwell of Tranströmer's apartment building in Stockholm as they wait to hear the news, as they had gathered and waited outside his home year after year. The film shows the announcement, and the journalists coming in to see Tranströmer, who lifts his left hand with wonder to touch the flowers they have brought to him. In addition to writing, he played classical piano, pieces written for the left hand, some composed just for him. His poetry conveys this strong sense of music at work in him, a legacy he had carried since adolescence. Tranströmer died at his home in 2015.

I chose Tranströmer because I have read him as though he has been speaking directly to me about my life. He knows the void, the edge of deletion, the whole world deleted, and writes at that verge. He is both terrifying and beautiful to read, even in translation.

In the play, I become a trace of the audible for these six writers, the director of an orchestra of voices, arranging and rearranging (from their writings) the positions of the speakers, their observations, questions, and riddles, as they grapple with the dual enigmas of existence and language.

*   *   *

After The Disaster
A Play in Two Acts

Cast of Characters

Emily Dickinson: A woman in her early thirties.

Janet Frame: A woman in her middle forties.

James Joyce: A man in his early fifties.

Barbara Suckfüll: A woman in her late fifties.

Tomas Tranströmer: A man in his seventies.

Robert Walser: A man in his sixties.

Scene

Austin Riggs library overlooking Main Street, Stockbridge, MA.

Time

The present; inclusive of the historic time of the writers.

ACT 1

SCENE 1

> Setting: *We are in the bay window end of the Austin Riggs library*, BARBARA SUCKFÜLL *and* JAMES JOYCE *seated apart, and* ROBERT WALSER *facing away, at a small writing desk.* EMILY

DICKINSON *is standing at the back of the stacks, and*
JANET FRAME *nearer the group, but also in the stacks.*

At Rise: Joyce looks at the books of David Rappaport, holding Beckett's
The Unnamable. The lamps are lit, and cast a soft light. Outside the
window, it is winter dusk, and a light snow is falling. Joyce stops reading, polishes his thick glasses, and faces the audience.

JOYCE: I throw this ended shadow from me . . . Endless,
                  would it be mine, form of my form? Who watches me
                  here?

TRANSTRÖMER: But often the shadow feels more real than the body.

JOYCE   [*aside to audience*]:   He lived at a little distance from
                  his body, regarding his own acts with doubtful side-
                  glances.

TRANSTRÖMER: I fell asleep in my bed / and woke up under the keel.

FRAME   [*peering around the stacks*]:   I rise disembodied from
                  the dark to grasp and attach myself like a homeless
                  parasite to the shape of my identity and its position in
                  space and time. At first, I cannot find my way, I cannot
                  find myself where I left myself, someone has removed
                  all trace of me.

DICKINSON   [*from the back of the library*]:   I, just wear my wings—

WALSER   [*looks up from writing with the stub of a pencil*]:   We
                  wear uniforms. Now, the wearing of uniforms simul-
                  taneously humiliates and exalts us. We look like
                  unfree people, and that is possibly a disgrace, but we
                  also look nice in our uniforms, and that sets us apart
                  from the deep disgrace of those people who walk
                  around in their very own clothes but in torn and dirty
                  ones. To me, for instance, wearing a uniform is very
                  pleasant because I never did know, before, what
                  clothes to put on. But in this, too, I am a mystery to
                  myself for the time being.

                  [*Walser writes again, looks up*]

                  Usually, I put on a prose piece jacket.

JOYCE   [*puts back the Beckett book*]:   The virgin at Hodges
                  Figgis' window on Monday looking in for one of the
                  alphabet books you were going to write.

DICKINSON   [*we hear the rustle of skirts, padding of feet, but see no one*]: The soul has moments of escape— . . . She dances like a Bomb, abroad

JOYCE   [*turning toward the voice, laughing*]:   Think you're escaping and run into yourself. Longest way round is the shortest way home.

DICKINSON   [*a bit testily*]: I dwell in possibility. The world feels dusty.

TRANSTRÖMER: The other world is this world too.

WALSER   [*looks around, turning in a circle*]: What else does the infinite consist of other than the incalculability of little dots?

                   [*he pauses, looks around*]

                   This reality. This treasure trove of in-fact-having-occurred-nesses.

JOYCE: Thus the unfacts, did we possess them, are too imprecisely few to warrant our certitude.

[*We hear a key in the door, and the overhead lights in the library go on.*]

SUCKFÜLL   [*looks up from her drawing*]:
                   The.Second.Devil.Was.On.The.Lookout.

                   [BLACKOUT]

                   [END OF SCENE]

SCENE 2

At Rise: Barbara Suckfüll looks around, pacing in front of the empty chairs. The others have fled, apparently. She lifts her drawing, fallen to the floor, and looks at it. She turns to the stacks to speak to the others.

SUCKFÜLL: That.Is.the.Washbasin.You.See.I.Have.Drawn.That.
                   Too.One.Time.
                   Too.And.Then.Today.The.Redhead.Brought.Cold.
                   Washing.Water.It.
                   Was.Too.Cold.What.She.Brought.Today.And.The.
                   Second.Devil.Was.
                   On.The.Lookout.I.Heard.That.Myself.Too.

                   [*We hear an ambulance siren in the distance*]

DICKINSON   [*speaks from the stacks*]:   The soul has bandaged moments.

FRAME   [*from the nearest row of the stacks*]:   Few of the people who roamed the dayroom would have qualified as acceptable heroines, in popular taste; few were charmingly uninhibited eccentrics. The mass provoked mostly irritation hostility and impatience. Their behaviour affronted, caused uneasiness; they wept and moaned; they quarrelled and complained. They were a nuisance and were treated as such. It was forgotten that they too possessed a prized humanity which needed care and love, that a tiny poetic essence could be distilled from their overflowing squalid truth.

WALSER   [*emerging with a scrap he tears*]:   I'm not here to write; I'm here to be mad.

TRANSTRÖMER: Once there was a shock / that left behind a long, shimmering comet tail.

DICKINSON   [*still in the stacks*]:   My cocoon tightens, colours tease. I'm afraid to own a body.

FRAME: I inhabited a territory of loneliness which resembles the place where the dying spend their time before death, and from where those who do return to the world bring a unique point of view that is a nightmare, a treasure, and a lifelong possession.

WALSER   [*nods to* FRAME, *sighs*]:   I would wish it on no one to be me / only I am capable of bearing myself / to know so much, to have seen so much, and / to say nothing, just about nothing.

DICKINSON   [*cupping her hand*]:   I could not weigh myself, myself. My size felt small to me.

TRANSTRÖMER   [*looking out the bay window*]:   And that which was "I" / is only a word in the darkness of December's mouth.

WALSER   [*smiles at* TRANSTRÖMER]: Houses, gardens, and people were transfigured into musical sounds . . . I was no longer myself, was another, and yet it was on this account that I became properly myself.

TRANSTRÖMER   (*to Walser*):   Fantastic to feel how my poem grows / while I myself shrink.

WALSER: The novel I am constantly writing is always the same one, and it might be described as a variously sliced-up or torn-apart book of myself.

DICKINSON   [*peers around a stack at* WALSER, *and retreats*]:   So we must meet apart- / you-there-I-here- / with just the Door ajar.

[*A door opens as Joyce comes into the library, and walks a bit unsteadily to the seating area.*]

JOYCE: I have met with you, bird, too late, or if not, too worm and early: and with tag for ildiot repeated in his secondmouth language.

FRAME   [*smiling, comes into view*]:   I had a cousin once who lived in your dictionary, inside the binding, and there was a tiny hole, which he used for a door, and it led out between trichotomy and trick. Now what do you think of that? It was only a few minutes walk to trigger, then over the page to trinity, trinket and trional, and there my cousin used to fall asleep.

JOYCE   [*sprawls on a sofa*]:   (Stoop) if you are abcedminded, to this claybook, what curios of sings (please stoop), in this allaphbed!

[JOYCE *sits up and shouts*]

'Tis as human a little story as paper could well carry.

DICKINSON   [*laughing softly, adds*]:   If it had no pencil.

[LIGHTS DIM]

[END OF SCENE]

ACT 2

SCENE 1

At Rise: JOYCE looks out the window, where it is snowing. He squints, and Frame comes to him.

JOYCE: I can't see. Is it snowing? And is there an establishment, I believe there is, called The Red Lion Inn, where we might imbibe a pint or two—ere the hour of the twattering of bards in the twitterlitter between Druidia and the Deepsleep Sea?

FRAME   [*shakes her head in disbelief*]:   How can we find a path in sleep and dreams and preserve ourselves from their dangerous reality of lightning snakes traffic germs riot earthquakes blizzard and dirt when lice creep like riddles through our minds?

WALSER   [*holds a brown paper scrap, a hole in the middle, peers through it*]:   Little clouds that look like bits of cotton wool are drifting before my windowpanes in the yellow blue.

SUCKFÜLL   [looking at her drawing]:   It.Is.Sunday.That.Is.the. Washbasin.You.See.I.Have.Drawn. Today.The.Redhead.Brought.Cold.Washing.Water. It.Was.Too.Cold.

JOYCE   [*places an overcoat around* SUCKFÜLL'*s shoulders*]:   The demand that I make of my reader is that he should devote his whole life to reading my works.

FRAME   [*frowns at* JOYCE]:   There was the frightening knowledge that the desire to write, the enjoyment of writing, has little correlation with talent. Might I, after all, be deluding myself like other patients I had seen in hospital, one in particular, a harmless young woman who quietly sat in the admission ward day after day writing her "book" because she wanted to be a writer, and her book on examination, revealed pages and pages of penciled O-O-O-O-O-O-O-O. Or was that the new form of communication?

TRANSTRÖMER   [*to* FRAME]:   The language marches in step with the executioners. Therefore we must get a new language.

JOYCE   [*reciting as he buttons* SUCKFÜLL'*s coat*]:   It had begun to snow again. He watched sleepily the flakes, silver and dark, falling obliquely against the lamplight. The time had come for him to set out on his journey westward. Yes, the newspapers were right: snow was general all over New England. It was falling on every part of the Berkshires, and outside in the Main Street of Stockbridge . . . He heard the snow falling faintly through

the universe and faintly falling, like the descent of
their last end, upon all the living and the dead.

DICKINSON   [*looking at the snow from the back window*]:   It sifts from
leaden sieves— / It powders all the wood.

TRANSTRÖMER   [*turns off the lights*]:   Are we Annihilated or just invisible?

[*Lights dim as they exit the library. We hear them descend the
stairs. They stand in front of Austen Riggs on the walkway and
seem a bit lost, hesitant to enter the town.*]

FRAME: One day we who live at the edge of the alphabet will
find our speech.

TRANSTRÖMER: Deep in the forest there's an unexpected clearing,
which can be reached only by someone who has lost
his way.

[WALSER *sits in a clearing, and lies down in the snow,
his face to the sky. The others gather around him.*]

DICKINSON: Such are the inlets of the mind. The gorgeous nothings.

WALSER: The sky, tired of light, has given everything to the
snow.

How small life is here, and how big nothingness.

[*They raise him up, dust the snow off his coat,
and walk toward the Red Lion Inn.*]

[BLACKOUT]

[END OF PLAY]

* * *

After writing the play, I sit in the bay window of the library at Austen
Riggs. It is quiet, that in-between time of day between the day's work
and the evening ahead of me. The patients have gathered for their
suppers, the doctors have gone home, and here I am, wondering about
the play I have composed. I can see and hear the writers clearly, imagine myself a member of the audience. Yet, they have only assembled
in my mind, this chorus of voices, these exchanges that spark across
the lines, the scenes, leaving me with questions.

What are the links between writing and speaking, between writing and drawing, and what is the relation of writing to time?

Writing is a gesture of the hand that leaves a trace of speaking. Early writing took the form of pictograms: a drawing of a bee next to a leaf might read as a homonym: belief. Our ears are tuned to such possibilities, these curious doublings of sounds and meanings.

If writing was at first a kind of drawing, a trace of speaking in graphic form, how did we come to alphabets? That ancient hodge-podge of graphic clues to represent speech sounds, then the early alphabets (gradually distanced from pictograms), carried human voices: sounds of speaking inscribed on stone, wood, papyrus.

Writing allowed voices to become timeless, and speakers to speak without being there. It makes sense to me that at least some psychotics would pursue writing and become memorable voices themselves.

Writing re-sounds the trace of music, something audible in the voice, yet something we cannot name in the registration of hearing.

What is this "psychotic kernel" of ineffable, intimate musicality?

This musicality in language, carried by the gesture of a hand and by the trace of a voice, is surely not unique to psychosis. "Of violin playing, Kandinsky observed that 'the pressure of the hand upon the bow corresponds perfectly to the pressure of the of the hand upon the pencil.' Only the pencil, however, leaves a trace" (Ingold, 2007, p. 143).

I think of Emily Dickinson writing on torn envelopes with the stub of a pencil in her skirt pocket, and Robert Walser's pencil method inside an asylum. They each left a singular "ductus" of the hand—a succession of moments in making a line, a gestural trace of voice.

In psychosis, the subject is confronted with questions of existence as pure enigma. What is her place in the world? What is it to be able to converse? What is it to love, and to love with one's body? What is the body and how to inhabit it? What is the worth of one's existence?

With nothing between himself and the void before him, the void after him, the writer becomes small, fades to nothing, paradoxically an immensity that fills the cosmos. In the play, there is nothing, the noth-ingness of existence, and then just the immensity of nothing.

Writing is sometimes an extension of the imaginary logic of delu-sion, as we hear in the lines of Barbara Suckfüll. Writers extend an address to a perverse Other who has taken over mind and body, creat-ing new code, a new order against the disaster of a lost place in language, as we saw repeatedly in the previous chapter. If we agree that delusion makes a place for the subject through a task or work that is completely original and is designed to fix a flaw in language *itself*, what is that flaw the psychotic subject encounters?

Here, I think it is useful to see how there is also a flaw in language that the neurotic structure confronts. For the neurotic, the flaw is a lack in language, the failure of language to say everything. We speak, listen, write, and language arrives in phrases, pinned down through a process of scansion as we anticipate meanings that only become clear at the end of a sentence. But each phrase, sentence, moment of saying, leaves something unsaid, and unsayable (Rogers, 2006). So we go on with revisions, elaborations, erasures, and questions, endless questions. If something does not make sense, we elide it, or decipher it. Desire unfolds in relation to a silent lack at the heart of speaking and writing. There is always "more".

But in psychosis the unsayable in language does not work this way. Confronted to questions of existence, she cannot find a way in speaking. She cannot scan particular fragments of speaking or writing, or decipher them. Perhaps she hears no voice, but something of the voice arrives in writing, and she hears in words *themselves* an enigma that cannot be explained. If there are no answers in the family or in society to questions of her existence, no conventional language that speaks to the place of the subject, what is left but to fix this flaw, to found a new language out of a place of impossibilities?

"The impossible to say, then the impossible to write. The real unconscious is something else. It can't be proved, it is not reached through logic; it emerges. That's why I have used the Joycean term 'epiphany'" (Soler, 2014, p. 57).

Writing as an art evokes and builds upon the impossibility to write, the "disaster" of language. It does so through strange moments of knowing that come upon us, in which we recognise something in language and outside of meaning. This was the case for Joyce, but is it not also the case for all great writers, all true poets? Is there any difference, then, between psychotic epiphany and a writer's epiphany?

The poet makes new language out of a legacy of received language and poetic forms, breaking new ground. The enigma of language in psychosis joins messages to codes, but not to a *given* code; speaking entails making a new language out of what were meaningless messages.

Code-messages and message-codes are produced in a linguistics of speech-in-action where the very fact of speaking, the very language acts of the psychotic subject, modify the language he uses to the point that the new language, modified by the language acts, can take on board the meaningless messages that were circulating outside any norm. (Laurent, 2012, par. 12)

At this point, I need Lacan himself to clarify the permutations of language I am trying to articulate here. In 1975–1976, Lacan gave an entire seminar year devoted to James Joyce, Seminar XXIII, *Joyce and the Sinthome*, using an old way of writing the symptom. This seminar changes how we think about psychosis, *what it is*, as well as the symptom, and writing as new language. Lacan shakes up his own way of thinking about language and psychosis in the first few meetings of that year.

Lacan declares that Joyce wrote in English in such a way that the English tongue no longer exists; it is now *lalangue*, a designation for elation in French. Is it possible for truth to become a product of a know-how (*savoir-faire*)? Lacan raises the question and answers it— No. Truth can only be half-said. Truth is equivocation. The sinthome cries out, "Mais pas ca—but not that!" (Lacan, 1975–1976, p. 5). The sinthome evokes the Real, outside the Symbolic of language, and is heretical.

Lacan goes further, questioning the status of the Oedipus. The Father, through the Oedipus, creates a symptom for the neurotic subject. This symptom is the decipherable symptom of the body, accessed through speech that carries unconscious meanings. The Oedipus as a fantasy, the truth of the symptom, and dreams—all can be deciphered through psychoanalysis, created for that very purpose.

The Father, Lacan says, also creates a symptom for Joyce—but it is not decipherable. Joyce has a Father, but he is entirely inadequate with regard to the question of existence, so much so that he ex-ists. In other words, he is outside the Symbolic. Joyce creates the Father with his art; he makes his family and his country "illustrious". He aims "to forge in the smithy of my soul the uncreated conscience of my race" (Joyce, 2005[1916], p. 253), as he says at the end of *Portrait of the Artist as a Young Man*. Lacan asks, "How can artifice explicitly aim at what is first presented as a symptom?" (Lacan, 1975–1976, p. 16). This question reverberates through the entire seminar in its trajectory from symptom to artifice and art, and a singular knot of four that creates a sinthome.

Lacan leaves us scratching our heads and reconsidering what he has taught about psychosis for a couple of decades, among them two crucial points. First, the foreclosure of the Name-of-the-Father is *not* a deficit; the Name-of-the-Father creates a symptom, after all, and its name is the Oedipus complex. Second, psychosis is *not* necessarily triggered in relation to foreclosure. The Father can be made to exist, as an art in writing, an art made of *lalangue*. And Joyce is not alone in finding this solution (as we see in the play with several of the writers).

What is the solution that psychosis seeks and finds in writing? As long as we are in the realm of *is this*/or *isn't this* schizophrenia, or paranoia, or mania with psychosis (identified through changing sets of criteria), we cannot begin to answer the question of writing in relation to psychosis. But what if we consider psychosis as an experience of enigma in language, *just that, only that,* and this enigma has implications for questions of existence, the real of the body, and the problematic of co-existence with others? Writing then gives a form for the "disaster"—the impossible to write. The development of a distinctive signature or voice transforms what I have called "incandescent alphabets" in this book to an art, an art that can be heard and acknowledged in the collective.

For someone who confronts questions of language in relation to questions of existence, writing grows out of the great enigmas of life. I am not talking about a young person who wonders what to do with his life, or how to come out as gay, or how to transition to another gender, as painful and anguished as those questions could become. I am talking about an experience of not being able to converse, to carry on in relationships with others or even consider sexuality—because one cannot inhabit the body. The body is strange, estranged, with an energy running amok, disorganising how it works. I am talking about wondering about how others speak, what words mean, how to "read" a joke or understand the context of how others meet, flirt, arrange their lives along the axis of being in a couple, or having a family. There is no social place for an individual who is subjected to language as a radical enigma. From this point, one might enter into psychosis, and leave the social link entirely. Or? Or come back from psychosis into a full life through writing.

Writing can serve as a know-how (*savoir-faire*), a singular solution to the enigma of existence. Each of the writers who assembled for the play assembled in speech. All of them faced insurmountable questions of existence. We know that both Emily Dickinson and Janet Frame had great difficulty being with others in every possible way (and created their own terms for relatedness). Others (James Joyce, Tomas Transtömer, Emily Dickinson) had supportive relationships within the family that made life, a writing life, possible. Some used writing itself to forge a name, a place, and a signature in language that spoke back to a collective, enlarging what language is, how it works, what it carries for humanity (James Joyce, Janet Frame, Tomas Transtömer). Others wrote as if to disappear from the world into writing (Emily Dickinson, Robert Walser), yet their writing speaks across time as utterly original. And if Barbara Suckfüll was lost in delusion, finding her way in language—One. Word. At. A. Time.—as if to keep track of language (as well as the devil), her word-drawings are so singular and stunning to encounter that they have made a way into contemporary art, such as the performance art created by Stuart Brisby. And Janet Frame considered language at the edge of its own crumbling, when it becomes useless. She speaks to the position of the subject in psychosis, but also, I think, to each one of us:

> The edge of the alphabet where words crumble and all forms of communication between the living are useless. One day we who live at the edge of the alphabet will find our speech.
>
> Meanwhile our lives are solitary; we are captives of the captive dead. We are like those yellow birds which are kept apart from their kind— you see their cages hanging in windows, in the sun—because otherwise they would never learn the language of their captors. But like the yellow birds have we not our pleasures? We look long in mirrors. We have tiny ladders to climb up and down, little wheels to set our feet and our heart racing nowhere; toys to play with. Should we not be happy? (Frame, 1962, p. 303)

Each of the writers in the play reinvents language, and yet that is what all true writers do. Still, for me (and after all, they assembled for me in the Austin Riggs library, that space just outside my office), the language reinvented is made to answer questions of existence. Overhearing them in a library filled with books concerning patients in real suffering (books about art, psychoanalysis, psychosis), I think of the patients who do not have access to any sort of treatment with dignity. Imagining my writers outside on the Main Street (where

Austen Riggs patients roam freely in the present day), I claim these six for my project on psychosis, even if they do not want that label. I do so to restore humanity through listening to that "psychotic kernel" in their words, and the elation of music in language for all of us.

NOTE

The sources for the voices in my play come from published works of the writers. I have taken the liberty to transform each scrap of writing into a voice, putting the material to work on behalf of speaking among themselves in relation to questions of existence and death, language and writing. Each writer becomes a character of my invention. In a few cases I have emended their words to make the dialogue run more smoothly, as noted below. Following the chronology of presentation, these are my sources:

Act 1, Scene 1

Joyce, J. (1986)[1922]. *Ulysses* (Chapter 3, Proteus, p. 408), H. W. Gabler (Ed.). New York: Random House.

Tranströmer, T. (2011)[1987]. After Someone's Death. In: *New Collected Poems* (p. 79), R. Fulton. (Trans.). Tarset: Bloodaxe Books.

Joyce, J. (2006)[1914]. A painful case. In: *Dubliners* (p. 134). Delaware: Prestwick House.

Tranströmer, T. (2006)[1987]. Winter's Code, I. In: *The Deleted World* (p. 21), R. Robertson (Trans.). London: Enitharmon Press.

Frame, J. (1961). *Faces in the Water* (p. 26). New York: George Braziller.

Johnson, T. H. (1958). *The Letters of Emily Dickinson, Volume I* (p. 236). Cambridge: Harvard University Press.

Walser, R. (1969)[1909]. *Jacob Von Gunten* (p. 26). New York: George Braziller.

Walser, R., Bernofsky, S., & Benjamin, W. (2010). *The Microscripts* (p. 67). New York: New Directions.

Joyce, J. (1986[1922]). Proteus. In: *Ulysses* (p. 424), H. W. Gabler (Ed.). New York: Random House.

Dickinson, E. (1961). The Soul has Bandaged Moments. In: *Complete Poems of Emily Dickinson* (p. 512), T. H. Johnson (Ed.). Boston, MA: Little, Brown.

Joyce, J. (1986)[1922]. Nausicca. In: *Ulysses* (p. 360), H. W. Gabler (Ed.). New York: Random House.

Dickinson, E. (1961). I Dwell in Possibility, The World Feels Dusty. In: *Complete Poems of Emily Dickinson* (pp. 715, 657), T. H. Johnson (Ed.). Boston, MA: Little, Brown.

Tranströmer, T. (2011)[1987]. How the Autumn Night Novel Begins. In: *New Collected Poems* (p. 119), R. Fulton (Trans.). Tarset: Bloodaxe Books.

Walser, R., Bernofsky, S., & Benjamin, W. (2010). *The Microscripts* (pp. 69, 70). New York: New Directions.

Joyce, J. (1939). *Finnegans Wake* (p. 57). London: Faber and Faber.

Suckfüll, B. (1996). In: Clausen, B. C., Jadi, I., and Douglas, C. *Beyond Reason Art and Psychosis: Works from the Prinzhorn Collection* (p. 175). Berkeley, CA: University of California Press.

Act 1, Scene 2

Suckfüll, B. (1996). In: Clausen, B. C., Jadi, I., & Douglas, C. *Beyond Reason Art and Psychosis: Works from the Prinzhorn Collection* (p. 175). Berkeley, CA: University of California Press.

Dickinson, E. (1961). The Soul has Bandaged Moments. In: *Complete Poems of Emily Dickinson* (p. 512), T. H. Johnson (Ed.). Boston, MA: Little, Brown.

Frame, J. (1961). *Faces in the Water* (p. 112). New York: George Braziller.

Walser, R. (1999)[1909]. C. Middleton Introduction, letter to Walser's editor, Carl Seelig (emended). In: *Jacob Von Gunten* (p. xv). New York: New York Review Books.

Tranströmer, T. (2001). After a Death. In: *The Half-finished Heaven* (p. 28), R. Bly (Trans.). Minneapolis, MN: Graywolf Press.

Dickinson, E. (1961). My Cocoon Tightens, Colors Tease and I'm Afraid to Own a Body. In: *Complete Poems of Emily Dickinson* (pp. 1099, 1090), T. H. Johnson (Ed.). Boston, MA: Little, Brown.

Frame, J. (1982). *To the Island: An Autobiography* (p. 99). London: Little, Brown.

Bianchi, M. D. (1971)[1924]. *The Life and Letters of Emily Dickinson* (p. 240). New York: Biblo and Tannen.

Tranströmer, T. (2006)[1987]. Winter's Code II. In *The Deleted World* (p. 21), R. Robertson (Trans.). London: Enitharmon Press.

Walser, R. (2013[1960]). The walk. In: *The Walk and Other Stories*. Croydon: Serpent's Tail, pp. 54–104.

Transtromer, T. (2006[1987]). Morning Birds. In: *The Great Enigma: New Collected Poems* (p. 79), R. Fulton (Trans.). New York: New Directions.

Middleton, C. (2012)[1982]. Introduction. In: *Robert Walser: Collected Stories* (p. xi). New York: Farrar, Straus & Giroux.

Dickinson, E. (1961). So we must meet apart. In: *Complete Poems of Emily Dickinson* (p. 640), T. H. Johnson (Ed.). Boston, MA: Little, Brown.

Joyce, J. (2012[1939]). *Finnegans Wake*. Oxford: Oxford University Press, p. 233.

Delbaeve, J. (1978). *Bird, Hawk, Bogie: Essays on Janet Frame*. Aurhus: Dangaroo Press, p. 71.

Joyce, J. (2012[1939]). *Finnegans Wake*. Oxford: Oxford University Press, p. 115.

Dickinson, E. (2014). If it had no pencil (PL 12) In Gilman, C. (2013) Curator *Dickinson/Walser Sketches*, New York: The Drawing Center.

Act 2, Scene 1

Joyce, J. (2012)[1939]. *Finnegans Wake* (p. 37, emended). Oxford: Oxford University Press.

Frame, J. (1961). *Faces in the Water* (p. 10). New York: George Braziller.

Walser, R., Bernofsky, S. & Benjamin, W. (2010). *The Microscripts* (p. 103). New York: New Directions.

Suckfüll, B. (1996). In: Clausen, B. C., Jadi, I., & Douglas C. *Beyond Reason Art and Psychosis: Works from the Prinzhorn Collection* (p. 175). Berkeley, CA: University of California Press, p. 175.

Ellmann, R. (1983)[1959]. Joyce interview with Max Eastman. In: *James Joyce* (p. 703). Oxford: Oxford University Press.

Frame, J. (2004[1984]). *An Angel at My Table* (p. 231), J. Campion (Ed.). London: Virago.

Robertson, R. (2011). The Double World of Tomas Transtromer, *The New York Review of Books*, November 10.

Joyce, J. (2006)[1914]. The Dead (emended). In: *Dubliners* (p. 168). Delaware: Prestwick House.

Dickinson, E. (1961). It sifts from leaden sieves. In: *Complete Poems of Emily Dickinson* (p. 311), T. H. Johnson (Ed.). Boston: Little, Brown.

Transtromer, T. (2011[1987]. Dream Seminar (emended). In: *New Collected Poems* (p. 142), R. Fulton (Trans.). Tarset: Bloodaxe Books.

Frame, J. (1962). *The Edge of the Alphabet* (p. 303). New York: George Braziller.

Dickinson, E. (2014). Such are the inlets of the mind (PL 10). In: C. Gilman (Curator), *Dickinson/Walser Sketches*. New York: The Drawing Center.

Bervin, J., & Werner, M. (2012). *The Gorgeous Nothings: Emily Dickinson's Envelope-Poems*. New York: New Directions.

Tranströmer, T. (2011[1987]). The Clearing. In: *New Collected Poems* (p. 118), R. Fulton (Trans.). Tarset: Bloodaxe Books.

Walser, R. (2012). Oppressive Light. In: *Oppressive Light: Selected Poems of Robert Walser*, D. Pantanoi (Trans.). New York: Black Lawrence Press.

CHAPTER SIX

Beyond psychosis: returning, remaining traces

W e all have the capacity to wonder about things, and, wondering, to invent new ideas about reality that become reality. That is not the mark of psychosis. Consider any enquiry and invention: poetry, art, mathematical proof, scientific discovery. We create what was not there before out of moments of rupture, inspiration, the odd passing thought, impetus, idea. Our invention lands into a social network that believes it, finds it valuable, can build from it, or at least admire it. The psychotic, however, not only invents something new, but also bears an enigmatic language concerning lived experiences outside of any social link that could recognise the terms of her language or invention. The new language, created to repair a flaw *in language itself*, to put order back into a world in which the perverse Other has wreaked havoc, can seal the psychotic into another reality. That new language encompasses both the disorder and the new order, and she follows *that* in reality. How does one return from such an experience in language? Because we *do* return, with and without medication, with and without psychotherapy or any form of treatment.

What traces of the experience of language in psychosis remain, and how secure is the return? Two of the accounts of psychosis from

Chapter One provide illuminating trajectories of returning, if we read the language closely to hear what changes and what remains.

Barbara O'Brien, the woman who took a Greyhound Bus across the United States in the 1950s at the behest of voices (O'Brien, 2011), recorded a glossary of terms, words that functioned as new language. The language came from her voices and repurposed ordinary words, for the most part, with singular definitions that sometimes introduced imaginary and strange ideas. A repeating word central to Barbara's experience was "Operator", defined as "A human being with a type of head formation which permits him to explore and influence the mentality of others" (p. 199). Terms such as "Latticework" seem more ordinary, described as "The structure of the mind of a Thing which results from habit patterns" (p. 199). This idea is not so strange or difficult to grasp in its meaning outside psychosis. Some words described mechanical means by which the Operators did their work, such as "Stroboscope, equipment used to probe and explore the minds of Things. Can be used over a distance of one mile, in a straight line" (p. 199). Then there was the phrase, "Shoot temples full of shack", delineated as "a process which prevents the use of the stroboscope" (p. 199). As in any esoteric language, words and definitions proliferated as they became embedded in a logical relation to one another. The terms of this language not only explained what happened to Barbara, but how it happened, by what means. Caught in its fine net of meanings and logical connections, one may well wonder how she emerged from her experience of voices and delusions.

Barbara not only returned to live a full life, the voices predicted her recovery. She writes, "I told both [a psychiatrist and psychoanalyst] that my voices had told me that I would be well within two weeks" (p. 162). She adds, wryly, "And the ability of the analyst to recognize the fact that a spontaneous recovery was on its way and the inability of the psychiatrist to recognize the same thing is worth emphasizing" (p. 162). It is clear, in retrospect, that her own unconscious guided her, using the voices:

> There was a very obvious awareness in my subconscious mind during the days that immediately preceded the cessation of the voices, that when the voices would cease, the mentality would be in a vacuum for a time and the organism, consequently, was going to need guidance on the outside. It was necessary that the dry beach be parked safely somewhere. (p.162)

There are several striking words in this brief passage. First of all, while Barbara makes an attribution to "my subconscious mind", it is her voices that guide her to the analyst. There is nothing repressed here that requires her to decipher meaning or direction. She refers to her mind as "the mentality" and her body as "the organism", as though her subjective experience of inhabiting mind and body has vanished, or diminished greatly.

Once she realises that the Hook Operators had been delusions, Barbara experiences what she calls "the dry beach". In her own words,

> For ten days, the dry beach. My scalp felt strained as if some nerve would break at any moment, but the interior of my head felt empty and dry, as if its cells had been hollowed out by a ruthless knife and replaced with a sandy shore. (p. 115)

She found the radio unbearable, did not remember how to read, forgot how to navigate walking in traffic in a city, could not follow or understand the plot of a film; her mind was blank much of the time and she slept a great deal, usually fifteen hours a night by her account. Then, on the eleventh day, her dry experience was broken by "a wave". She describes the experience:

> The wave fell, disappeared into the sands and left on the beach a thought. I remembered suddenly the purpose of the traffic signals and what the green and red lights meant. I passed a newsstand and saw a newspaper headline which announced that a star had fallen from a window. The dry beach contemplated the headline with mild surprise. How could a big thing like a star get into a window? A wave cascaded gently on the shore and I realized suddenly that the star was probably a Hollywood star. *Death of a Salesman* said a movie marquee. The dry beach blinked at the marquee and speculated vaguely that a Sales man might be a native from some country named Sales, probably in Asia. Then a wave broke and I remembered that I had read the play and I was aware sharply of the name of the country in which the salesman was a native. I was grateful for the waves. The waves could remember, deduce, apply insight. The dry beach could not. (p. 117)

At this point, Barbara begins to recognise and remember the world she left behind, but the process of returning is not voluntary. While she was caught in delusion, her voices directed everything she did, taking over her thoughts as well as her acts. In the months after the voices vanished, Barbara experiences "waves" as thoughts or insights, as well as signs, omens, and images that direct her acts, her speech, and her writing. All come from an external source, outside herself and her intentions. In analysis, she learns to attribute these external signs and influences to her unconscious. But her unconscious is not repressed, to be painstakingly uncovered, deciphered, giving up its secrets and logic almost unwillingly; rather, her unconscious takes on the function of the Operators, directing her in the face of questions and situations she simply does not know how to navigate alone. Via the analyst, she has a space in which to speak and to sift through her experience of these sudden, external messages, which are disconcerting to her, as much *and more* than the Hook Operators had been for her.

Barbara describes a kind a persistent blankness in the early days of the analysis; she had nothing to say spontaneously, or, for that matter, nothing in response to the analyst's questions.

> And then, unexpectedly, one day after the analyst had asked me something, a wave cascaded abruptly onto the beach. Surprised, I absorbed it and passed it on to the analyst. In my youth, I said, I had entertained ideas about writing fiction and had put the ideas away with other toys. Startled at hearing me say anything, the analyst surveyed me a second, and suggested immediately that I write something. (p. 118)

Barbara went out, bought paper, and began to write. In her account, she was not aware of what she was writing, and as soon as she stopped for the day, could not recall anything she had typed. She writes,

> I was composing as fast as I was typing . . . I typed for two hours and sat back to read what I had written. The material was a little difficult for the dry beach to follow but the story seemed to be about some woman and some man and some people the woman knew who were getting ready to do something to the man. (p. 118)

She wrote daily for two hours, and though she could not keep track of time, she arrived to write precisely at 2.00 p.m. each day, as if directed by an external "Something". She wrote an entire novel in about thirty hours in this fashion.

Barbara describes the process: "The words came from nowhere, shot down through my fingers, and appeared magically on the paper" (p. 120). She realises that famous writers and musicians sometimes describe their own creative process in these terms, too, as though directed from without, as though their work had been written or composed by itself. Her analyst explains that the process is unconscious, and what is unfolding through her unconscious (the waves, the writing) is simply more evident than is usually the case.

As I read Barbara's narration of the time after the voices left her, what stands out is for me is that her unconscious is not only externalised and cut off from her intention and volition, but utterly transparent in its directives. She identifies to the position of the "dry beach", and the "waves" offer thoughts and whole sentences to her. She describes writing as though it happens without her participation. Except for the fact that she is the typist, it is as though language speaks or writes by itself. She identifies these experiences as coming from her unconscious because she is in analysis, but the analysis does not decipher her experiences. Perhaps there is nothing to decipher here. Yet, Barbara comes to realise that her unconscious can act on her behalf. After all, the Hook Operators directed her at the start of her journey, demanding that she bring her portable typewriter, a heavy item to carry around when travelling by bus.

It interests me, too, that Barbara's explanation for what happens to her in these weeks and months of returning to "reality" (and making a life again) echoes her experience of psychosis. "Something" beyond her own thinking, intention, and even her capacity to comprehend what is at stake, reminds her how to navigate the world, directs her writing (and time-keeping), shows her the way to a job as receptionist, predicts situations, and tells her what to say, and, when she runs out of money, helps her to win money against the odds in Las Vegas by showing her which numbers to choose. This "Something" is able to think in her place and direct her life, and, when she opposes it, this "Something" becomes more insistent. At the end of this period, she explains, "Something abruptly unscrewed its odd attachment and stopped extending" (p. 125). Here "Something" sounds perilously close to the activities of the Hook Operators working through the Imaginary body invasively. Although Barbara calls "Something" her unconscious, it is not the unconscious as a chaining of signifiers, connecting elements from the unconscious to lived history and puzzles of sexual desire. In fact, as she puzzles over what was the cause of her schizophrenia (and her Freudian analyst argues it was a deficit in sexual experience), she disagrees with him. She finds nothing about her sexual life connected to her schizophrenia, or to her unconscious for that matter.

I think she is right to protest these ready-made interpretations. She experiences language as invasive, as a parasite in her mind, even during this time of recovery. For a long time after the voices stopped, she is not alone with herself, with her own thoughts. For a long time, she is unable (of her own accord), to reshape her life, make decisions, and piece together why it was that she became psychotic. In fact, Barbara puzzles over what happened to her and its consequences for the last third of the book. She returns to reasoning, as she knew it before her psychotic experience: "And then abruptly, overnight, the strange equipment was put away in storage, the regular machinery was hauled onto the dry beach and connected" (p. 137). This passive voice perspective and the allusion to machinery moved around and connected reads as an extension of the experience of "Something" that intervenes; it happens to her. None the less, Barbara regains a sense of herself:

> With the return of reasoning came the return of emotion. I awoke one morning, sat down to breakfast, and found myself thinking and feeling. Before I finished my cup of coffee, I was grasping for the first time just what had happened to me and what it had done to my life. (p. 137)

As Barbara begins her life again in California, far from the small town where she grew up, went to college, and took her first job, she sees her unconscious as

> that fine friend of mine which has manoeuvred me so adroitly in insanity, had manoeuvred me, also in sanity, into resigning my job and into writing notes to myself to remember that I must never return to the company for which I had worked. (p.140)

She comes to see that Hook Operating was going on all around her in her former office, and that she had escaped it. She then decides to take a job in California as a writer of publicity, and, in doing so, finds herself in a "horribly familiar" office environment in which "there was no way of protecting yourself from these hatchet men except by picking up a sharper hatchet and learning how to use it" (p. 195). Although she learns some strategies for self-protection, Barbara realises that if she were to rise in the organisation, she would have to "become an expert at swinging the hatchet, clutching and fondling the knife" (p. 196). Instead, she resigns, and takes another job at the bottom of the pecking order, determined to make sure "I never became overly bright about learning the business" (p. 197). She does not want to risk becoming a Hook Operator.

At this point, as the book ends, I wonder about what she encountered in those offices that posed a massive threat. The hatchet men and their knives can be read as metaphors, of course, but they are all too real for her. There is no principle, no recourse to advice, help, or trustworthy authority to assist her in these situations, so she resolves never to rise in any organisation. I hope it was a strategy that worked for her, because we do not know. Her book was written under a pseudonym; we know nothing of the actual author, or her continuing life-story.

Psychoanalysis did not cure her, perhaps because it was not modified to fit her experience. After all, Freud invented psychoanalysis for neurosis. Yet, her time with a psychoanalyst, one who listened to her and trusted her unconscious, no matter its eccentric formations, provided Barbara a bridge from psychosis to a gradual, supported period of returning to the world, to work, to a life outside insanity, a life of her choosing.

Yet, I cannot help but wonder about that very thing that triggered her psychosis; some baffling, threatening situation repeated with each office job. Barbara used what she learnt from the Hook Operators to navigate the world, rebuilding her life in relation to them, their directives and their language, but her new life carried traces of her experience in psychosis. Those traces, in fact, became her unconscious guides. However, such traces are of "the Real"—outside the Symbolic—and they can, at least potentially, lead back to madness.

Whitney Robinson, the young woman who experienced a mental breakdown in her first year in college, writes in her memoir about her confrontation with the voice of a demon and changes in her experience of language, which devolves, at times, into poetry. She recounts, with a sense of irony that perhaps only the young can invoke with such a keen edge, her encounters with the mental health system: hospitalisations, medications, dire warnings about her future, and life in a half-way house. Her story of returning from psychosis (Robinson, 2011) reads as a story in progress. Yet she insists on finding a way to live in the world, return to college, and make her way without relying on medication.

Several turning points in this narrative depict Whitney's return as a process of finding a link to a future she can embrace, and a connection to her own humanity, which has been compromised through her experience of psychosis and its medical treatment. Whitney battles with her psychiatrist about medication throughout the book, alternatively taking various antipsychotics, and refusing them. She depicts Dr Caspian as someone who does not know her experience, but as a kind man who worries about her. She describes to him the side-effects of her medication as "nausea, terror, dry mouth and trembling" (p. 128). He tries to convince her that she will get used to the medications and their side-effects, but, sharp-eyed adolescent that she is, Whitney says that none of the older patients has become used to such side-effects. When she collapses from a higher dose of the same medication, Dr Caspian tries a second antipsychotic. He is clear with her that she will have to take these medications all her life. She writes about the effects over time: "I think it's the drugs that are causing this, quite literally turning my world gray. They are not just antipsychotic, they are anti everything. I do not feel scared or violent, but I also do not feel" (p. 221). She is caught in a bind: if she takes the medication, her world is gray, she can barely function, and the demon is kept at bay. But, when she goes off the medication, feels alive once more, and is able to think, the demon returns. She is also implicated in his return, and his dismissal, as we will see.

Whitney signs a consent form for electroconvulsive therapy and then revokes her agreement, and when she cannot be talked into changing her mind, she is transferred to a half-way house residence. There, patients maintained on medications learn basic life skills. She describes her fellow patients:

> Most of the patients fall into one of two categories—the broken ones who trace hieroglyphs on paper and rant about nanotechnology in the rice pudding, and the silent ones who drift like hungry ghosts through a world they can neither escape nor manipulate. (p. 191)

One cannot read such a sentence without seeing the intelligence that formed it. But, to her carers, Whitney can only learn a few simple rules, and must be watched, medicated, and reminded how to behave in an appropriate way continuously. She comes to believe this pattern will be her future, and that her doctors have ". . . earned the right to ticker with my chemicals" though this makes her "slow, unimaginative, too literal to be seduced by demons or other creatures of poetry and dreaming" (p. 192). This, for me, is the saddest chapter in her book.

Then, something unexpected happens, which devolves into a crucial turning point. Whitney sits in a group of patients in an exercise of writing letters none of them will mail, and she writes a letter to her demon. She throws her letter into a recycle bin later, and one of the doctors discovers it. Dr Hunter calls her into his office and tells her about another patient who went on to graduate school in physics. "I teach some very bright students," he says, "and even among them you would be exceptional" (p. 203). At this point, Whitney turns away, "Please don't. I'm not. Please don't offer me the world. I'm not ready to take that weight again" (p. 203).

Yet, even before this point, her letter to her demon carries the message that she is finished with him, and she knows it. She has written,

> So if it was only me you were trying to destroy—well played. Beyond that, I can only confess that sometimes my deeper structures wish you were still observing, that you could bathe me once more in the pure light of delusion and fill the part of me that was born empty. Sometimes the scar tissue is not enough. Signed, Your Other, the one left real as we reach the end of this. (p. 206)

The Other, for Lacanian analysts, is the site of language itself, the treasury of signifiers though which we speak and are recognised. The language of the demon—his poetry—infiltrates and stays in Whitney's language. He has the status a delusion, but also of being Real, real enough to address as an entity in a letter. After reading the letter that has been returned to her, Whitney knows it is the end with the demon. She writes:

> For the second time I awaken in the dark, frozen in a night-terror state of arousal and unreality. I feel him breathing, forbidden fruit hot copper exhale, and wait trembling for him to speak. But something in my mind is beyond his authority now—the neurons to which he whispers are drugged and stupefied. When I feel him fading away,

I am seized by a paroxysm almost as violent as when he came, but of my own making. He isn't squeezing my lachrymal ducts; the tears splashing onto the sheets are those of a free agent. (p. 208)

These two experiences, that letter that forecasts the end with the demon, and a recognition of her intelligence (the opening of another future), set the stage for the next step Whitney takes. She discovers a stack of pamphlets announcing a contest for student research on mental illness. She nabs one, tucks it away, and gets to work. A month later, she hears from the medical director that she has won the contest. The staff at her treatment facility are baffled, but Dr Hunter is not surprised. Whitney reads her paper, which includes aspects of her own experience, at a grand rounds, and receives her award. Following this recognition, the staff begin to see her in a new light, and they have higher expectations for her.

In short, she returns to living at home, and then re-enters college. She also chooses to come off her medication, finding her way with the clarity of mind and energy such a choice opens. At her father's suggestion, she tries many alternative strategies, even meets with a shaman, which seems to her and her family better than anything else on offer.

What changes, and what aspects of psychosis remain with Whitney? In a sense, everything changes for her as she goes back to college, and we see this as she calculates her risk in daring to be part of humanity again. On the other hand, her experience of psychosis (and the possibility of identifying with it as a disease that excuses her from trying) stays with her as a shadow.

Everything is changing, changing, falling apart, putting itself back together again. Suddenly, I'm afraid and want to go home. I want to have a disease, to be exempt. If I said I can't take this, I can never be one of these bright and normal creatures, if I were to collapse . . . people would understand. It's shocking how easily everyone accepts excuses from me now. But after all this it just wouldn't be a very poetic ending, and I don't have any better criteria by which I determine how to live. So in a fairly inconsequential action that nonetheless requires more of me than anything yet, I enter the room and find a seat among my classmates. (p. 235)

Her subjectivity shines in this passage, her choice to do something that seems "inconsequential" with far-reaching effects. In the afterword to her book, Whitney tells her readers that she has been hospitalised again since the publication of her book. She has tried medications and stopped, graduated from college, and dropped out of graduate school.

What has changed for her then, really changed? Writing was a way to record her experience, but I think it was more than that; it formed a new purpose for her, a way with language. She writes, "Words burn in me and I try to express them. I may desire silence, but that's not the hand I was dealt" (p. 238). She has made a destiny out of the traces of her experience in psychosis, and it has ignited a desire to write. It is her choice, not something imposed.

And yet, and yet, she knows (as anyone who has inhabited psychosis knows) that language, what we make meaningful and what we experience as real through it, *has* been imposed on us.

> Demons surround us. In this way, they are much like words, omnipresent—in lecture halls, in chatrooms, in pine forests, in bus terminals . . . we never escape them. They occupy no physical space, they have no meaning independent of their hosts. Parasitic, without mercy, our constant shadows . . . they force us to fall, stagnate, become. They make us interesting, they make us doubt. They form our souls from an undifferentiated light. (p. 238)

What remains in Whitney's language that carries over from psychosis? She does not dismiss demons as unreal, but takes her experience as singular, a knowledge gleaned from an unforgettable experience. Furthermore, she links that knowledge of demons with language, "they are very much like words, omnipresent". Again, I am reminded of how hard it is for most people to understand how deeply we are formed of language and live with what has been imposed on us, from infancy. But for those who have lived psychosis, it is easy to know (and to say), that language is "parasitic, without mercy", and it works as a charged, luminous force in us. "They" in the last line of Whitney's book refers back to words, but words have been linked metonymically with unseen demons, which form us "from an undifferentiated light". As I read this line, I think here is where delusion carries truth, not just for Whitney, but a truth of what it is to be human. It is the kind of truth that cannot be separated from what is elusive, poetic, in language. And in my mind, her desire to write links Whitney to the writers and poets in the play, "After the Disaster".

* * *

Language, the arc of its trajectory into psychosis and back, carries what Lacan, in his late work, called the Real unconscious. What returns in language as Real could not be thought, spoken, or considered by the psychotic. Yet, that unnamed legacy, outside any form of symbolisation, is at the heart of the psychotic's delusion, her remaking of language in language. Might it also be her way back to the ineffable truth of experience? That, too, will come in language, language with new permutations connected to the social link. I know this well through my own experience.

Like Whitney, I returned from psychosis with fierce determination to come off and stay off medication. In my senior year of high school, I experienced something of real freedom from hallucination, and completed two years' work in one, graduating with my class. I was astonished that it was possible to study, but, even more than academic success, I was surprised to find friends who wanted to be with me after I had been so radically cut off from any social life. Then, in my first semester away at college, my voices recurred quite abruptly. It took me six years to complete my undergraduate degree, living at home once more, seeing a psychiatrist and a psychologist weekly. During these years, nothing truly disrupted my building a delusion, and I continued working on a celestial language. I was in and out of hospitals for short periods two to three times each year in the face of repeating crises, and took antipsychotics in the hospital, stopping when released. In my sessions with a clinical psychologist with psychoanalytic training, I discovered the first connections between events of my lived experience and the command voices that led me to act, repeatedly attempting to take my own life. This work of psychoanalytic psychotherapy saved my life, I think, but it did not take me out of psychosis.

During these years, except when in the midst of a crisis, I could speak coherently, even articulately. Very much as Barbara O'Brien reported, I sensed that Something was directing me, orientating me (in my absence) to navigate the everyday world. I heard voices and phrases imposed over my own thoughts, and sometimes I scrambled directions as I tried to reach where I needed to go. I found that I was unable to draw in perspective. I had no interest in sexual relationships, and could not bear to be touched. I looked years younger than my chronological age. Yet, day in and day out, I navigated the world of college, then graduate school, with success.

Then I had a particularly severe crisis in my late twenties and I lost all ability to speak comprehensibly, to recognise even my family, and to keep track of time. I was so disorganised that I cannot recount much about that time spent in a private psychiatric hospital. I did not get better, and months later, as my insurance ran out, my doctors recommended a state hospital. But my sister, my advocate in this situation, refused that option. After my release from the hospital, I was still in very bad shape. I lived with a former professor and his family because I could not live by myself. I went to see a psychoanalyst who was known for his success with psychotics. I was sceptical, despite his reputation. However, he became the analyst who accompanied me as I changed my entire life. Dr Bloomenfeld understood that what others "called gibberish was a language and he trusted my voices" (Rogers, 1995, p. 127). He trusted what I saw, heard, and knew from inside psychosis. From that beginning, we made our way slowly together to discover the truths of my earliest experience, and, in doing so, I lost all the symptoms of psychosis. At first, I was incredulous, fully expecting the next crisis, but I was alone with my thoughts and, for the first time, I felt lonely. Gradually, I found a ground of sanity upon which to build a life as an adult and complete a degree in psychology, move to Harvard to do research on girls' psychological development, join the faculty, and begin a private practice working with children and adolescents.

The constructions I made through psychoanalysis eventually connected my psychotic crises to intergenerational signifiers that had never been anything other than floating words, disconnected from lived history, and my subjective experience (Davoine & Gaudillierre, 2004). In this sense, I was able not only to return from psychosis to make a life, but also to turn psychosis inside out with respect to language and the unconscious, making a different relationship with language: what it is and how it works. I can identify five changes or moments with respect to language, and I want to note them here because they might be of some use to those who treat psychosis through psychoanalysis.

First, here are the details of my lived experience of delusion. Psychosis entails profound changes in the body. Foreign objects and beings invaded and divided my body and kept surveillance over me. Splinters from the wood of a stake, implanted in my arms at night when I slept, could be lit if the Cardinals of the Church saw that I was making a universal, Celestial Language. I lived with a burning in my arms and the fear of my whole body burning. Also, an internal tube of poison, released again and again into my intestines, filled me with the fear of dying—and the antidote to the poison was translating scrambled messages by imposed deadlines. I experienced my body as taken over by external forces—keeping surveillance of my work with language—daily and nightly. When I was subjected to doubts that I would succeed fully in this work, I experienced a level of chaos I cannot describe even now.

I had to find a place to say what has been impossible to say, with another human being. That person also needed to be someone who knew how to receive what I was saying. For me, this was a psycho-analyst who was not daunted by psychosis. The objects that roamed my body, taking me into a space–time outside the social link, were vestiges of something Real at stake in my early life. They held the truths of my most intimate experiences, which I thought had set me apart—irrevocably. This became clear through the work of my first, and most crucial, analysis. I did a second analysis much later, with further changes with respect to language.

In that first analysis, I worked to find connections between my experience of language and the objects that invaded my body, con-structing a past that I had never named before. After ending that ana-lysis, I never again experienced madness, but I did experience some fleeting symptoms, mostly having to do with difficulties navigating time and space. Then through another analysis, decades later, I went further. In that work, I learnt that the particular objects that had invaded my body in psychosis were linked with an unnamed (as if cut out of history) intergenerational pattern. I was able to find that pattern in signifiers from my dreams, and discover that dreams could be deci-phered, bringing me a new knowledge, a different kind of knowledge that was always open to question and reinterpretation.

From the time I was young, I wanted to be writer, and I wrote: poems, stories, and, later, books. A signature of poetic, lyric writing crosses all forms and is part of my writing to this day. But it was my own experience in psychoanalysis that opened the way for me to become a writer.

At the heart of my life had been an attempt to re-make language. It threw me into chaos, and into repeated hospitalisations. I worked for years to translate everything, every sound, even creating an incandescent alphabet that spoke volumes in a single letter. I followed the voices that arrived out of the blue. The Real of language took over my mind and body. It organised me and disorganised me. But my experience of language has changed dramatically. What changed with respect to language were five "moments"—some happening in a matter of weeks, others taking years.

The first moment was a realisation that something was strange in *my* use of language. It had two faces, this strangeness: mistakes with words, and metaphors I did not hear as metaphors. These changes began in my first analysis, when I was not long out of the hospital. I moved from epiphany (too much meaning born out of bits of nonsense) to questioning how I was using language—and my world changed. I wish that I could describe exactly how this happened. I began to hear mistakes in my speech, especially if someone else pointed them out, and I could laugh at them. My analyst also heard and formed metaphors using the signifiers in my own speech. I did not appreciate them as metaphors. Drawing from my speech, he said things I had never heard said before, never put together before. For example, he described me as "the girl with the blue lenses" (Rogers, 1995, p. 163). Blue became linked to infancy, to true seeing, and to a refusal to give way on my truths.

As the voices faded and vanished, I learned to inhabit silences. I was alone in silence. Although I thought that people spoke in ways that killed language, saying things they did not mean, using careless and worn out phrases, it was difficult for me to carry on simple conversations at certain junctures. I did not know the rules of the game. Gradually, I became aware that something was missing for me, a gap so large it was the size of a crater. *The second moment* of my new relationship with language entailed coming to terms with the fact that I simply did not know many common, cultural points of reference. And, although I have learnt a great deal and become fluent, conversing about common historical or cultural references remained for a long time like speaking a foreign language.

The third moment in my passage out of psychosis had to do with hearing the play of negativity in language, the impossibility of saying things directly. In my early years of work as a psychologist treating children, I noticed negations in their speech: "I don't know", "it doesn't matter", "I don't care". Negation disperses what it undercuts and turns it into a proliferating offshoot of what has been negated.

Language becomes divisible: we hear, and we do not hear but register—two modes that adumbrate each other. This is the way language
transmits what is inaccessible otherwise. In other words, language
itself carries "the unsayable" (Rogers, 2006). Psychoanalytic listening
depends on this realisation, which allowed me to work with children
and, later, with adults on the couch.

The fourth moment began when I realised that I had great difficulty
learning another language. I saw that I had one way of proceeding:
memorisation. And I could not have been *chosen* to be a translator of a
celestial language, a central part of my delusion that I had retained,
because I was not very good at languages. I also realised all translation
is a betrayal of the original—something is *always lost* in translation. For
a short time, this realisation, which shattered my delusion, threw me
into a kind of crisis. I could not speak of it. I had dreams that came like
messages, and I began to read the world as if what I happened to see or
hear were addressed to me directly. I knew that I could either follow
these messages, or find a way to distance myself from what I was experiencing and examine it. I chose the latter, writing a piece of fiction, and
the strangeness of that time passed. I also worked with the fiction in
relation to analysis, and came to see that the Other of my psychosis
was not, and could never have been, translatable.

I attribute each of the moments of change in my conception of
language, what it is, what it does, to psychoanalysis. In this way, I was
able to listen through gaps, dreams, acts, erasures; listen to what is
disavowed; listen to language as if it were foreign and strange. It was
all a kind of ear training in psychoanalytic listening. From the Other
side of the couch, I wait for some truth to emerge through slips, holes,
mistakes, speaking as ghost, whisper, trace, or symptom. I have, in a
long trajectory, earned the ears to hear the unconscious in ordinary
language.

It was through the later and final analysis that I realised *everything*
I had experienced in psychosis (even voices imposed from without)
had its origins in me, connected to other lives before mine, and to
things that had been transmitted across generations and had never
been named, said, or acknowledged. It was an astonishing discovery
to realise that what I experienced as external was produced from my
unconscious, and had been transmitted to me across generations. This
fifth moment utterly changed my relation to language and to psychosis.
I knew then that the voices were not "out there" somewhere, waiting

to return. There is no Other beyond language itself, and what it creates in us as effects. Yet, my voices had brought me vital truths, and those truths could live in language (language as poetry). What is most alive in me works through language but beyond anything that language can carry. Truth can only be half-said, as Lacan taught.

Several years ago, writing in my study in Ireland during the summer, I conjured the figure of my father, to discover that I had to write him as a construction to be able to make use of him.

Ghost:

He stood in the doorway and asked me, "What are you writing?"

He was a balding man with glasses, and now he pushed them up on his nose (of this gesture, I am not certain; I am not even certain that he wore glasses). He took a chair and sat down in my study.

It was only then that I recognised him. He was my dead father, whom I had not seen since I was five years old. I recognised his voice.

I asked him, as if he could tell me, "Look, can you see a voice? Spelling out alphabets in the air, drawing letters, one by one—can you see a voice spelling something you must sit down and try to write? Do you think that's possible?"

He did not answer, but wiped his glasses on his shirttail, the glasses I was not sure he was wearing.

"I don't know what it is I'm writing. Something to do with the beauty of music in language."

He nodded and said nothing. I thought I saw a glint of blue lightening in his black, black eyes—but maybe not, maybe his eyes were dark, and unanswering.

"Are you going to go on writing it?" he asked me.

My language now works through metaphor. I am not literally conversing with a ghost, and this ghost is not my father's ghost, but a character I have created. And this bit of dialogue, its continuation, depends on moments of uncertainty about him, which leads to more writing.

We make a world out of words, and mistake what language carries as reality. I am still unsettled by all the ways we use words to justify our acts, and, in doing so, become blinded to the actual trajectories of our acts, their incalculable effects. Our dreams whisper something else in our ears: a nub of nonsense, a puzzle that will not be solved easily. I am on this side of language. In fact, I have learnt to trust these whispered bits of nonsense so much that I have dared to write single, disconnected lines, to accompany abstract paintings, drawings, and prints. The lines seem to come out of the blue. At first, I was afraid that writing bits of nonsense might open me again to psychosis, but I have been writing nonsense in little sketchbooks daily for several years now, and remain quite outside psychosis.

In the end, this passage from psychosis to a metaphoric use of language, from language as a delusion made of imposed elements to language as traces that move around a vortex of silence, leaves a kind of truth in its wake. For me, this truth comes through writing, and especially through poetry. It is never complete. It carries the Real, the Real connected to language. For what language cannot carry, I turn to painting and to the wonderful accidents of printmaking.

Psychoanalysis has made this relation to language possible, has made this ground of lucidity.

*   *   *

As I explicate these versions of returning from psychosis, Barbara's, Whitney's, and mine, I want to consider how Lacan, late in his teaching (in the 1970s), introduced several ideas about psychosis (*the sinthome*, the *Real unconscious*, and the *Father of the Name*) that extend and also revise his earlier teaching.

But before I explore how Lacan reconsiders psychosis, both extending and revising his ideas, it is useful to review his thinking about psychosis in the 1950s. In *Seminar III, The Psychoses, 1955–1956*, Lacan argued that there is a signifier foreclosed in psychosis, and it concerns the *Name-of-the-Father* (Lacan, 1997[1981]). The concept *Name-of-the-Father* refers to what integrates a subject into shared normative and social language. Accepting the *Name-of-the-Father* implies that a subject can live his life in relation to norms and laws that, in a given culture, orientate human interactions and relationships (acceptance might include rebellion as a way to reshape and claim ideals). In either case, the subject finds ideals and answers to fundamentally existential questions such as what life means in the face of death, and the question of how people should relate, particularly sexually. The ideals connected to the *Name-of-the-Father* provide an orientation around the fundamental uncertainty associated with these points of identity, enabling the next generation, as desiring beings, to formulate their own questions and choices.

However, in psychosis the *Name-of-the-Father* is foreclosed, and, therefore, the psychotic subject not only lacks answers to these existential points of identity, but, more fundamentally, he has a different relation to the Symbolic (Lacan, 1997[1981]). Through gaping holes in the Symbolic, hallucination attempts to formulate the position of the subject as impossibility, as a bit of the Real. From time to time in childhood, something profoundly strange or perplexing occurs; the Real imposes itself; the child cannot name it, talk about it, or make sense of it. He or she just returns from it and goes on with a life that resembles normality. Then, most often in adolescence or early adulthood, when it becomes pressing to situate oneself as a subjective actor in the social fabric, the holes in the Symbolic open into more profound and lasting irruptions of the Real, and into psychosis as a lived experience.

In an essay from 1957–1958, "On a question prior to any possible treatment of psychosis" (2006b), appearing in English in *Ecrits* (Lacan, 2006a), Lacan proposes a structural distinction between the neuroses and the psychoses. For Lacan, the difference hinges on a distinction between repression and foreclosure (Freud's *Verwerfung*); in psychosis the Name-of-the-Father is foreclosed. This means effectively that what cannot be spoken as a subjective position returns in the Real. What returns imposes itself as a voice addressing the psychotic and telling him something about himself: "the signifying chain imposes itself, by itself, on the subject in its dimension as voice" (Lacan, 2006a, p. 447). What is spoken seems to come from without. Hallucination is both Real and called forth by whatever is foreclosed, unspoken, and incomprehensible in the signifying chain. The voice (or unspoken message) is foreign, externalised, and strange. The person who is in psychosis builds a delusion, formulating an explanation from such charged, significant experiences of strangeness. Lacan's idea of foreclosure of a crucial element of the Symbolic in relation to questions of existence creates, as an effect, this strange experience of the Real. Foreclosure is the incapacity to signify one's own experience as a subject in relation to questions of existence as a human being. Foreclosure becomes evident through the presence of unchained signifiers; in other words, hallucinated experience comes in at the very point where language as a Symbolic system becomes derailed.

Yet, all language fails in so far as signifiers circle the Real as a hole; we are never finished with speaking. When signifiers circle the Real, language works through metaphor, and the Real leaves a sense of mystery, of the ineffable. For example, Tomas Tranströmer (2006 [1987]) writes, "The only thing I want to say / gleams out of reach / like the silver in a pawnshop" (p. 199). Poetry evokes the Real as the unknown, the unimaginable; we read it and recognise what it points towards as a metaphor, a bridge from the known world to the unknown. How different is Tranströmer's use of language here, the artful way it evokes the Real as an unknown element, in comparison to language that is saturated with the Real, as an external, received, imposed knowing? Remember Dan's brother, David? We do not comprehend what he is saying but there is the pattern of speech interrupted, followed by sonorous, repeating phonemes that do not read as metaphors: "I'm not going to [he stops, looks away]. On the second day, the second coming is coming, by God. Orange is inside God, God isn't yellow, He likes oranges. He made them all; after all, God is God. My hands are turning orange and my body is going on exhibit at the l'Orangerie". These words do not circle the Real. The Real imposes itself on speaking and signification is shot through with impossible holes.

If we leap forward in time some twenty years to Lacan in Seminar XXIII thinking about knots, the Real, the father (in a new way), and the unconscious, the ground of how we consider psychosis shifts. In this seminar, *Joyce and the Sinthome* (1975–1976), Lacan uses an old word for symptom to forge a new figure in psychosis—the writer as one who has the know-how to re-make language by taking it apart—thereby making, for himself, a unique name. I would need to write another book to do any justice to Lacan's thinking about psychosis, Joyce, and the intricacy of Borromean knots and their geometric topology, a branch of mathematics. That is not this book, and neither is it my purpose. I only want to glean a few key ideas that would explain some possibilities and limits for returning from psychosis. I shall begin with Lacan's revision to the Name-of-the-Father.

Lacan says in Seminar XXIII that one can very easily do without the Name-of-the-Father, "provided that one makes use of it" (Lesson X, April 13, 1976, p. 11). This takes some unravelling. In Seminar XXII, *Real, Symbolic, Imaginary* (1974–1975), Lacan departs from the Name-of-the-Father as the agency of the law and linchpin of the Symbolic, and the father as a metaphoric function in relation to the Desire of the Mother. What, then, becomes of the function of the Father? Lacan creates certain permutations on the father and his function. It is the Name-of-the-Father that produces a symptom, and the symptom is the Oedipus complex. This, of course, pertains to neurosis, to those who have accepted the Name-of-the-Father. The Name-of-the-Father creates a symptom, but we can do without the father, if we can make use of him, Lacan tells us in *Joyce and the Sinthome*. Lacan asserts that knotting (of the Borromean chain that holds together the Real, Imaginary, and Symbolic in neurosis, but slips apart in psychosis), can be repaired via a sinthome.

Colette Soler (2014) clarifies that in psychosis it is not the signifier of the Name-of-the-Father that is missing so much as the Father as "not his signifier but his saying" (p. 143), his saying in a crucial function of nomination. Soler sums up Lacan's position about the knot, the sinthome, and the Father: "Lacan ends up by asserting that this knotting takes place via the nominating saying, sliding from the Name-of-the-Father to the Father of the Name" (p. 153). She continues, "To say that the Father names is already to say his function is not the function of metaphor" (p. 155). She reminds us that Lacan said that naming or saying is event. And an event has the status of an act. Nomination is not, itself, a signifying function, Soler underlines. In other words, unlike signifiers taken up in the Other, this saying of the Father, this Father of the Name, is not in the desire or discourse of the Other. Rather, "saying" links the Symbolic and *jouissance*. Any deconstruction of language (such as done by Joyce, or created at the end of analysis) leads to a reconfiguration of the Real as a *saying the Real*, where saying is an event.

Soler shows how the psychotic can make his way with language without access to the signifier of the Name-of-the-Father. "In response to the subject's question, Che vuoi?, the Symbolic makes a hole, an irreducible hole. . . . Names come from the hole of the unconscious. The hole, Lacan says, spits out the Names of the Father" (p. 156). These Names of the Father knit some bits of our speaking to the Real. The implications are profound, and I shall try to say something further about this link between the Real and the Symbolic in the next two chapters.

The father has changed. He is nomination, Father of the Names. A father is a version of the oedipal symptom, too, but no longer functions to secure a place in the Symbolic because the Symbolic cannot be isolated from the Imaginary and the Real. The nomination father functions as a sinthome, and one can do without the Name-of-the-Father, as Joyce does, by allowing the unconscious to spit out "the Names of the Father". *Jouissance*, the Real, comes into speaking and writing then, and is part of the ineffable kernel of real *jouissance* at the heart of language, not only for the psychotic, but *for all of us*. This is the stuff of poetry, the neological unconscious that cannot be deciphered, but registers its sonority on the body. Read a poem many times and see that you cannot sum it up, say what it says, but it will *produce sayings in you*—new sayings that are also ineffable, and register on your body.

How can we make use of these two distinctive trains in Lacan's thinking: the foreclosure of the Name-of-the-Father in the Symbolic and its effects, and the Father of the Name, the Father of saying, who, out of the hole in the Real that language made, takes on the function of nomination? These two ideas from Lacan help me to make a provisional set of conjectures, conjectures that are open to question. Foreclosure of the Name-of-the-Father leaves its mark: the subject will encounter repeating, baffling situations she cannot grasp. Once subjected to psychosis as madness, as a mental breakdown, language *itself* bears the mark of that foreclosure: it is invasive, a parasite in the mind and body, and words are saturated with the Real—as we see with all three examples in this chapter.

It is possible to make a provisional, short- or long-term return from psychosis as madness—with or without medication—provided the psychotic can find someone who acts as a anchor (for a time), someone who believes in and upholds the humanity, subjectivity, and knowledge-as-lived-experience of the psychotic. But the experience of psychosis as madness can impose itself again if the subject meets a situation that is, once more, utterly baffling and threatening—if she cannot escape these effects by leaving the situation. This is precisely the situation of Barbara O'Brien at the close of her book.

Writing seems to be a way through and beyond psychosis for some subjects in psychosis. But writing, *in itself*, does not appear to be enough to prevent the re-emergence of psychosis once it has been triggered. Whitney Robinson is an exquisite writer, and yet writing her book did not prevent another crisis and hospitalisation.

And psychoanalysis? It was not made for psychosis, and will not turn the psychotic subject into a neurotic. However, it is my experience (my personal experience) as well as my conjecture that if the analyst takes the function of the Father of the Name, *the function of saying as event*, by drawing on the psychotic's delusion and speech *to say something Real*, it is possible for a psychotic subject to begin the long traversal of the loss of delusion. If this happens, he will discover a new relation to language in which the Symbolic makes a hole around the Real; the Real becomes a mute hole, and speaking can never be entirely true, the truth entirely said. When this happens, the Real becomes inaccessible, except in its traces and effects, and the individual is truly free of the triggering of psychosis as madness. I return to this idea of the analyst who takes the function of the Father of the Name in the final chapter.

CHAPTER SEVEN

Psychosis and the address: new alphabets and the enigmatic Other

W hat does it take for someone who is entirely caught up with his own projects and concerns, whose true interest lies elsewhere, to find a way into speaking? "For it is difficult to speak, even any old rubbish, and at the same time focus one's attention on another point, where one's true interest lies" (p. 27), Samuel Beckett writes in *The Unnamable* (1994[1951]).

How do we listen to individuals in psychosis who might yearn to speak, but cannot find the words to convey their most vital experiences? And, when someone has lost faith in speaking, what compels her to try again? How do we receive language that sometimes sounds incoherent or eccentric with respect to ordinary, unstated norms of speaking? What does it take, on the part of the listener, to receive the psychotic subject as a subject *worth* listening to, worth working to hear? And how can we respond to individuals in a psychotic crisis, as well as those at the edge of that experience? Finally, how might we listen to someone after a crisis in ways that open up conversations into spaces of exploration and discovery, surprise, and sometimes even laughter? These are questions I have formulated especially with clinicians in mind, but they may pertain to anyone who simply wants to listen. Yet, to enter into conversation with individuals who have traversed psychosis, one must consider a different experience of the world, and a specific position in the address of the psychotic subject. One also must become curious about the experience of psychosis in all its permutations.

I start with someone who speaks, but is difficult to understand. Language in psychosis, constructed as an *effect* of an encounter with a ghastly, enigmatic Other, can become structured by an address that is confusing and frustrating to follow. Although the psychotic speaker might be willing to answer questions, his address can become impossible to follow. While he addresses the person in the room asking questions, he seems to speak to another (one or many persons or entities listening in), entities that keep track of what he says, and even dictate what to say.

I consulted with a young psychiatrist recently about how to listen to patients in crisis (he had no training whatsoever in this regard). He recorded the following conversation with his patient, which baffled him. He began by posing a question to his patient, a woman in a psychiatric hospital in the midst of a crisis.

How did your visit go?

It was good that the matter of about one hundred million years ago was solved. There were too many stars falling, and the number of them we counted didn't count up to them all. I knew that.

Are you saying your visit with you sister was good?

The stars didn't live long enough to for us visit them. The Pale-maker signed their deaths and they were counted and executed.

Oh, that sounds frightening.

No, it wasn't loud. It happened about 2,300 light years ago, in the night when the Pull people moved through us, leaving deposits and depositions and, I should not be saying this. They are listening in, and telling me *what* to say. It's a trap, and the Klevins will collect us when it's time to count and collect anyone who talked.

The patient turned away from him then, muttering to herself about nosy people to be avoided. The doctor, to his credit, had attempted a conversation. But, even as the speech of the patient shifted to another reality, another universe, he continued as though they were both talking about the patient's visit with her sister. Finally, as though he *could* understand and empathise with what the patient reported from that other reality, the psychiatrist offered, "Oh, that sounds frightening". But the patient did not understand his remark.

On the patient's side, she never discusses the visit with her sister, but introduces a received knowledge that the stars were not all counted. The visit then refers to stars that could not be visited, because they did not live long enough. The patient explains that an entity, the Pale-maker, "signed their deaths". The patient continues to clarify her position, answering the doctor's statement, "Oh, that sounds frightening", with "No, it wasn't loud". Notice that this is a direct reply, but it is based on the mistaken idea that the psychiatrist refers to an audible sound. Finally, after saying a little more about what has happened (at the level of a cosmic disaster), the speaker admits that she should not be talking; others are listening and laying a trap.

The patient speaks to the doctor, but her address lies elsewhere, I would argue. The patient, seeing that someone asks her a question and waits for her to answer, answers with *what she knows*, and even elaborates on what she knows. That this patient knows something she is trying to convey seems lost on the young psychiatrist. And, in the end, he seems "nosy"—a bother to the patient, who has become impli-cated now among those who have "talked". The address, I believe, is to a perverse, all knowing, and destructive Other. The patient stops speaking, acknowledging the Klevins as ones who count and collect those who have spoken (metonymically linked to the stars that were counted, collected, and executed). The patient depicts herself in grave danger.

From the patient's point of view, what does she know? First, "There were too many stars falling, and the number of them we counted didn't count up to them all. I knew that". And she also asserts a solution has taken place: ". . . the matter of about one hundred million years ago was solved". Finally, she establishes a timeline: "It happened about 2,300 light years ago, in the night when the Pull people moved through us, leaving deposits and depositions . . ."

So many questions flood my mind as I review this material (which I present verbatim, with the psychiatrist's and the patient's permis-sions). Is this patient among the "we" who counted the stars? And, what happened to the stars that escaped the count? Did they live? Who were the Pull people? When she says "us" as in "the Pull people moved through us", does she refer to herself in a group, or to herself as many entities? Finally, what was the problem that needed to be solved in the first place? But to pose these questions would be to take her knowledge seriously, to enquire about her position, and to ask about what is implied but not stated. Too often when doctors "listen", it has the effect of shutting down the psychotic speaker, so that what she knows becomes unspeakable, beyond exchange with others. We do not usually ask questions about experience and knowledge with patients who are psychotic. Yet, asking these questions might be a better way of proceeding than imposing our ways of conversing, point of view, and theoretical frameworks.

Yet, the psychotic risks a great deal to speak. Here is a letter addressed to me as the writer of *The Unsayable* (2006), which came with a request in an email:

> Dear Author of The Unsayable,
>
> I had a sleepless night, I went to the stage door of a performance that was announced to me concerning the Bervermin. One of them had a false seizure in my leg, and my body seized up. I could not move, so I missed Life that night, and am now officially Dead. I spoke about this to the New York Police and to the King of the Bervermin. They put out a warrant for my arrest. Since that day anyone can enter my body in hundreds. Total chaos reigns now. They are against real freedom of speaking and know nothing of the unsayable. I heard them on the radio making another announcement: moles are eating my liver. I could feel their sharp teeth. If I go to the hospital, the Bervermese will be there, waiting. Perhaps you can assist with this difficult situation.
>
> Sincerely,
>
> Man, NO LONGER LIVING

In this short note, I hear how the psychotic bears witness to invasions into his body. He utters what he has heard, language imposed through two announcements and their consequences: a body that has changed, incomprehensibly—first it seizes so that he cannot move, then moles eat his liver, and he reports that he can feel their teeth. It is not possible to overestimate the extent to which the body becomes a host for the malevolent Other of the psychotic. And, since the body of the psychotic is not only open to invasion, but to impossibilities such as existing in multiples ("anyone can enter my body in hundreds"), or being dead yet writing a letter, it can be difficult to credit these references regarding the body. Yet I do, because *not* to credit them would be to silence this writer, effectively. I also hear in this letter an appeal to authority ("the New York Police and to the King of the Bervermin") that merges with a new threat ("they put out a warrant for my arrest") and distrust ("If I go to the hospital, the Bervermese will be waiting"). This man has lost faith in representatives of the law and does not know where to turn.

I notice that there are signifiers that repeat: life, liver, NO LONGER LIVING, Bervermin, Bervermese King, and, perhaps, in this chain we can add the moles (as a species of vermin). I do not think, however, that it is possible to trace a trajectory from such signifiers to multiple meanings and to an idea that has been repressed. They repeat, as though for emphasis, as collected bits of music in speech. Perhaps the most coherent message in this email is a request to be taken seriously. The man writes, "They are against real freedom of speaking and know nothing of the unsayable". "They" might refer back to "The New York Police and the King of the Bervermin" or to the hundreds who have entered his body. He has addressed me as "Author of The Unsayable", giving me an opening to reply from that identity.

I responded this way:

Dear Man, NO LONGER LIVING,

What you say has a basis in your own experience. I receive the message that you are in chaos and bodily anguish. I live very far from you, but can recommend someone in your city, Dr. _____, someone you might meet and speak with, a person will want to hear the unsayable, as I do. He is all FOR freedom of speaking.

Author of the Unsayable

I discovered later that they met and had begun to meet regularly. But, of course, I know nothing more—their work is confidential. It was crucial for me to discern a request, and to reply to the terms of the address, both to me (in a position as writer), as well as an indirect address to a menacing Other based on the patient's experience. I imagined the courage it took for this man to email me in the midst of his chaos and desperation.

But, even if we want to listen, the problem arises of how to orientate in a different universe of speaking. I offer three additional examples.

Each of them restores subjectivity to the psychotic—on his terms, the coordinates of his world and "reality"—and also extends his world just a little.

Perhaps the most striking instance of sheer respect for another human being lost in his own world comes from the art historian, John MacGregor, who writes about his visits with Dwight Mackintosh in *Dwight Mackintosh: The Boy Who Time Forgot* (1990).

> Watching him draw, all day, everyday, one is invariably astonished by the utter certainty with which he proceeds, by the absolute authority and conviction of his line, and by the undeniable authenticity of the resultant images. Pen in hand, he is unmistakably an artist. (p. 13)

Mackintosh (who appears in Chapter Three) worked in the last years of his life in an open studio, Creative Growth Center in Oakland, California, a setting designed for handicapped individuals. This was not a therapeutic milieu, but a place to make art. He had no physical handicap, and his mental trouble was both evident and not entirely clear. Was he mildly mentally retarded, neurologically damaged, autistic, or psychotic? After fifty-six years living in mental institutions, it was impossible to tell. In his old age, he made striking, original, complex, beautiful images crowded with writing that was unreadable. He spoke in short phrases, appeared lost in his own world, profoundly withdrawn, lacking interest in communication. He depended completely on others to navigate his day-to-day living. What a contrast to see the work he produced!

As I read MacGregor's book, I realised gradually that he not only recognised Macintosh as an artist, but as a man whose originality should be respected and preserved. MacGregor argued that Macintosh was outside the world of art: he did not make "art" for any audience, but created for his own reasons, and never even looked at his finished work. His work bore the mark of "the strange and extreme artistic manifestations we associate with Outsider Art" (p. 16). His art was also, curiously, outside of time. He drew buses with spokes on their wheels from the early years of the twentieth century, and he drew himself as a series of boy figures. His writing, MacGregor also noted, contained dates from the early 1900s when Dwight was a boy. At one point, teachers at the Creative Growth Center tried to get Macintosh to copy from magazines and use conventional painting techniques; they asked that he finish his images, and stop writing all over them.

MacGregor protested in this way: "Had this 'art school' mentality been imposed successfully on Mackintosh, his work would have been permanently undermined and his significance as an artist obliterated" (p. 37). I read that sentence several times. It is a shining example of upholding the outsider's position, guarding masterful images made not for the art world, but from a drive to create bound up with a timeless world of fantasy, a world of little boys with huge penises, floating and multiplying bodies, unreadable scripts with undeniable significance for the writer, complex transparent vehicles, and, in the last years of his life, absolutely stunning use of colour and line. MacGregor did not pretend "understand" what Mackintosh thought, what meanings his work had for him, and, to his credit, MacGregor, trained as a psychoanalyst, did not impose interpretations beyond a few moments of brief speculation. What comes through is a profound respect for one elderly, severely limited man making astonishing images.

I think of all the ways that family, friends, and clinicians work for, and hope to change, those who have entered psychosis (as another reality) and live there, stay there. I, too, have done this. But, perhaps there are times when it is most human (and deeply respectful) to become a presence that simply and fully accepts a lasting affliction and the gifts that come with *that* version of things.

I do not mean, however, that we should give up listening at any point. Interviewing hospitalised schizophrenic patients in Denmark, Bert Rosenbaum and Harley Sonne present a detailed framework for listening to patients. Their book, *The Language of Psychosis*, published in 1986, opens up both psychotic experience and creative therapeutic interventions with chronic schizophrenic patients. Rosenbaum is a psychiatrist versed in Lacanian psychoanalysis, and Sonne is a linguist. Their research included rich examples of interviews with patients, as well as samples of their writing, accompanied by close textual readings. It is instructive and humbling to read their exegesis of first, second, and third person shifts in discourse in these texts, alongside their interpretations of fantasy and the Imaginary body in psychosis. What struck me again and again was the presence of an interviewer who was open, interested, and non-judgemental.

In the following extract, a patient speaks to her interviewer about reading the newspaper aloud so that twenty different planets can listen. She mentions various departments as well as "trisks and svilts" (her made-up words) who listen in. Here is what unfolds.

I: Can you talk to these trisks and svilts?

P: Well, they don't speak to anyone. But a wire can be attached to them, then they're able to speak.

I: Hm. Have you attached . . .?

P: People have been put into them. Then they can speak.

I: Hm.

P: No, I don't speak with them. We're not allowed to speak very much. A tape explains it to us.

I: Hm. That means that you don't think you are speaking yourself? It's a tape that's speaking?

P: Yes, it's a tape that's speaking.

I: Hm.

P: There isn't anything . . . it's not people speaking. It's a tape that's like in the Parliament, there they also have, I don't know who, they have tapes there too. They talk . . .

I: They have tapes in the Parliament?

P: Yes, there . . . they have tapes they talk on. But it's the same, you know, trisks and svilts, you know, it's the same, when one has tapes, it's the same.

I: Oh . . .

P: Yes, they don't really care when one has tapes. They don't pay any attention to that. (Rosenbaum & Sonne, 1986, pp. 12–13)

The interviewer asks about the patient's experience, wanting to grasp *her* position in this Other world she inhabits. The patient elaborates, telling him that the trisks and svilts ". . . don't speak to anyone. But a wire can be attached to them, then they're able to speak". He asks if *she* attaches the wire, and the patient seems to ignore that question, but explains, "People have been put into them. Then they can speak". The interviewer just makes one of those gentle, listening noises, "Hm"—and the patient returns to his earlier question, "Can you talk to these trisks and svilts?" in a direct response: "No, I don't speak with them. We're not allowed to speak very much. A tape explains it to us". The interviewer is not pushy, and this might have given this patient the space to decide what to say and to return to the question of her own accord.

The interviewer infers her experience of the tape. He guesses, "That means that you don't think you are speaking yourself? It's a tape that's speaking?" Unlike making conjectures with a neurotic, who might adopt the point of view of the clinician to please him, careful guesswork, open to the patient's correction, can be useful with psychotics. The patient confirms, "Yes, it's a tape that's speaking".

I would ask different questions about this tape, what it is and how it works, but this interviewer asks about the patient's subjective experience, not refuting it or dismissing it. Considering the great enigma of what she is being subjected to, the patient has become isolated in a singularly original network of ideas, sometimes comprising idiosyncratic words. The conversation reported is a genuine exchange, breaking into her profound isolation.

Rosenbaum and Sonne present a case towards the end of their book to illustrate two phases of a treatment for hospitalised schizophrenic patients who have lived in psychosis for a very long time. In the first phase, the therapist moves from being outside of the patient's address to finding a place in the psychotic's discourse in second person perspective, referred to as "you", even if he is included in the delusional system. In the second phase, the therapist can ask questions about the delusional system in relation to subjective history. The result is not a cure, but a space created in which subjective history can begin to exist alongside delusional experience. It is worth reading.

Lacanian analysts in Quebec City, Canada, have taken the treatment of psychosis farther. Willy Apollon, Danielle Bergeron, and Lucie Cantin established a space for treatment of young psychotic adults through psychoanalysis in 1982. Named for its address in the city, "the 388" is a unique place in the world. Cantin (2009) describes what it offers young people:

> More than a hundred patients receive a comprehensive and long-term treatment there, which includes intensive treatment of the crisis, thereby assuring them of an alternative to hospitalization. Ninety-six percent of the clientele is composed of persons suffering from schizophrenia and other psychoses, the majority of whom present, upon their arrival, an extensive psychiatric past of multiple hospitalizations and diverse therapeutic attempts . . .

Since its creation, we have wanted to offer a *treatment* to the psychotic by proposing an analytic work to him wherein he is engaged, guided by the psychoanalyst, in reconsidering his entire psychic life. The objectives of this treatment are the profound reorganization of the mental universe, the reappropriation of speech and subjectivity, the disappearance of the psychotic symptomology, the resolution of the stakes governing the triggering of the crises, the restoration of an autonomy in personal and social functioning, and the return to an active life of civic participation (work, studies, volunteer work, artistic work, familial responsibilities). (Cantin, 2009, pp. 286–287)

This treatment centre has had considerable success in precisely these terms; over 65% of young people with serious psychotic disorders complete an analysis and live full lives subsequently. Anyone interested in the psychoanalytic treatment of psychosis would do well to visit and learn from these analysts and the professional staff of the 388. I want to remark on just a small part of that work, a short example in which the analyst relies on the psychotic's dreams to make a bridge to a subjective history and a logic that will come to undermine the delusion.

In *After Lacan* (Apollon et al., 2002), in a chapter aptly named "From delusion to dream," Cantin writes about the treatment of Mr T. After giving a detailed case history of childhood and adolescence, Cantin presents Mr T's dreams. At first, his associations take up elements of his delusion. Here is the third dream he brings:

I see a cleaning lady dressed in white. She is rather pretty. I don't know how she did it, but she got me with her face. It is as if she had gained my confidence. She goes by the bed. I see her and then I completely lose sight of her and it is as if she were going through my forehead. (p. 99)

In his associations, Cantin tells us, Mr T speaks of seduction as a trick to paralyse him. He also speaks of the woman going through the third eye. But the analyst does not leave him in this flow of ideas. Cantin writes, "I then intervene and ask him whether he has any childhood memories related to his forehead. He recalls an accident where his brother suffered a forehead injury" (p. 99).

This way of listening to delusion first, then to dreams, has a specific purpose: to promote another logic against the closed logic of delusion. Here is Cantin once more:

The intervention takes the form of a question. In asking him whether the forehead is related to childhood memory, something different is introduced into a system that until then has been closed up. "The woman who goes through his forehead," a representation provided by the dream, is traced back by him in his associations to an element of delusion. There, its meaning is fixed, closed: the forehead is the place of the third eye, the spiritual eye. It is as if the dream-work brought nothing more, as if it didn't come from an Other scene, from a place Other than his imaginary universe. The analyst's questioning, however, brings back the subject's history—and even more importantly, it establishes for the psychotic subject that dream work is governed by laws *other* than those of consciousness or imaginary creation. At the next session, Mr. T. relates a dream and then, for the first time, produces associations linked to elements of his history. (p. 99)

Working with the logic of the dream and distinguishing it from delusional logic, the analyst intervenes to open up and sustain the logic of the dream. Gradually, a new "saviour"—knowledge from experience of analysis—will change the experience of psychosis itself and create new possibilities in this young man's life. But such a result depends on establishing a civic and clinical space that will support a psychoanlytic treatment (a lengthy psychoanalytic engagement), and the presence of a team of professionals working together to create an alternative to medication and hospitalisation.

* * *

In all these examples, I am referring either to those caught in a delusional system for a long time, or young adults who have been in and out of hospitals in quite disorganised states. But it is not at all uncommon for people to experience long periods of stabilisation in relation to psychosis that can take various forms.

In the second part of this chapter, I explore listening as the psychotic periodically moves in and out of disorganised states and crises; as well as orientating ourselves when the diagnosis is not clear, and when psychotic symptoms emerge in a transient way and resolve quickly. I realise as I write that there is a trap in writing about psychosis, and I have fallen into it (as have most of my colleagues). The very repetition of the phrase "the psychotic" creates a misunderstanding of what psychosis is, in fact. Psychosis is heterogeneous in its manifestations, and there are multiple trajectories through

psychosis as an experience. Some people recover full sanity spontaneously, and others recover after treatment, and still others manage to
find a way out through their own ingenuity. In the final part of this
chapter, I return to psychosis as a structure, not as a form of madness,
but as a human experience of the body, language, and the social link.

How do we understand various possibilities, trajectories, points of
stability and vulnerability, as we listen? Is it possible to learn something new about what psychosis is and what it might open as a life
trajectory, including a compelling life of both love and work? What are
the social networks that make such life feasible, possible, even as
someone moves in and out of psychotic crises? Elyn Saks, author of
The Center Cannot Hold (2007), writes about her experience of multiple
crises that took a devastating form early in her adult life, beginning
when she was a Marshall Scholar at Oxford University. Saks was
hospitalised repeatedly. In the UK, she saw a Kleinian analyst, Mrs
Jones, who gave Saks a space to speak terrifying fantasies, but did not
in any way modify analytic technique for psychosis. Saks continued
to experience psychotic crises, but, in time, she finished her degree
and gained entry to the Yale Law School. At Yale, the pattern of crises
and hospitalisations repeated. In the USA, her experiences with
psychiatry were horrifying to her: she was held in four-point restraints
for long periods, forced to take massive doses of antipsychotic
medication, stripped of choice, dignity, and hope. Saks never forgot
those experiences. Her work as a lawyer (yes, she finished her law
degree) involves setting legal limits to such inhumane measures. She
is Professor of Law at a prestigious university and a research clinical
associate of psychoanalysis. She has also married, after discovering
love and sexual experience for the first time in her forties. How did
she build such a life? We might well wonder.

Saks had access to speaking about her experience frankly throughout her adult life, both in treatment relationships and in a few
wonderful friendships. She has also taken various antipsychotic
medications, and to this day continues with medication to regulate the
worst of her symptoms. Yet, her life trajectory also depends on strong
friendships. In college, she found a small group.

> Kenny, Margie and I often hung out together. . . . We had dinner
> parties (happily for me, the others knew how to cook), listened to
> music, talked about our studies and our friends, and mostly laughed

a lot. . . .. I'd never been a giggly girl, but something about these people made me feel light-hearted most of the time. (p. 45)

This cluster of friends, and, later, other steadfast people, including life-long friends like Steve, gave Saks a place of belonging in the world that she might find again following even the worst, most disorganising and terrifying, crises. Her friends knew of her schizophrenia and acted as anchors when she teetered at the edge of a crisis. Her husband, Will, a man who accepted her fully, also helped Saks to steer through crises. These people were not part of any treatment team; they loved her, admired her, enjoyed her, and believed in her. Her capacity to find, nourish, and repair friendships, alongside developing a life trajectory with a contribution to society, has held for decades.

For Saks, there are limits also. She takes medications that have side-effects. For her, travel is disorganising, as is sex. She limits both because they disorganise her in space and time, and in her body. She is careful. She is not beyond psychosis. Her life is a full life of tremendous courage, and her work, which protects patient choices in the treatment of schizophrenia, has meaning for Saks herself and for many others. She has made a satisfying, rich life *in* psychosis, provided we think of psychosis outside delusion, and, on any ordinary day, a person both seeming and being quite sane.

But there is a curious erasure of time in psychosis. For some people, like Saks, this loss of time involves periods when she cannot live in the world, but must have time out from the demands of living to find her footing again. One does not make up for this lost time; it is lost. Others might find that it is difficult consciously to track their experience in time, and, therefore, hard to plan, to follow through, and to navigate the demands of daily life. How do we hear someone who is struggling to continue with some semblance of managing her life when it is becoming increasingly impossible, not because she is subjected to voices, or even disorganised language, but because she cannot reckon with *where she is* in relation to time, self, and the body?

Louis Sass and Josef Parnas (2003) describe subjective, conscious experiences of psychosis from interviews with patients who have experienced a first crisis. Their conceptualisation unifies the heterogeneity of schizophrenic symptoms as having roots in "certain disturbances of self-hood or self experience" (p. 427). Sass and Parnas argue that schizophrenia is a disturbance in ipseity, defining ipseity as "the

experiential sense of being a vital and self-coinciding subject of experience or first person perspective on the world" (p. 428). They analyse
two complementary aspects of ipseity disturbance: on the one hand,
"hyper-reflexivity, exaggerated self consciousness involving self alien-
ation", and, on the other hand, "diminished self-affection, diminished
intensity or vitality of one's own self-presence" (p. 429). These two
aspects effect not only a sense of self, but also perception of the world,
resulting in "a disturbed hold or grip . . . and a loss of salience or
stability with which objects stand out in an organised field of awareness" (p. 429).

Sass and Parnas argue that ipseity disturbance contrasts with
normal experience. "In our everyday transactions with the world, the
sense of self and sense of immersion in the world are inseparable; we
are self-aware through our practical absorption in the world of
objects" (p. 429). Furthermore, they argue that our "capacity to have
intentional acts stems from embeddedness in the world, along with
a tacit, pre-reflective self-awareness or ipseity" (p. 429). They point out
a contrast in psychotic experience. In *"hyper-reflexivity*, something
normally tacit becomes focal and explicit", and with *"diminished self-
affection* what was once tacit is no longer a taken-for-granted selfhood"
(p. 432). The result is a changed experience of presence and absence—
an absence of organisation that comes with small erasures of subjective being, and the presence of one's thoughts and feelings as foreign,
as vivid and present, but not part of one's own experience.

Another way to think of what Sass and Parnas assert is that
changed aspects of perception make it quite plausible and possible for
something strange and perplexing to happen to the subject. If there is
a gap between an individual's sense of self and the flow of her consciousness, aspects of subjectivity could become reified and externalised: no longer part of self, they become strange and puzzling. The
logical extension of such a state is that inner experience appears to
come from outside and becomes impervious to one's personal control.
What we see in psychosis is a profound self-alienation, beginning with
subtle, but disturbing, changes in perception.

Parnas (2000) interviewed schizophrenic patients following a first
crisis and hospitalisation in the hope of learning something about
what happened just *before* a first crisis. The patients reported profound
changes that were difficult for them to describe. Here is the summary
of one interview.

Robert, a twenty-one-year-old unskilled worker, complained that for more than a year, he had been feeling painfully cut off from the world and had a feeling of some sort of indescribable inner change, prohibiting him from normal life. He was troubled by a strange, pervasive, and a very distressing feeling of not being present or fully alive, of not participating in the interactions with his surroundings. He was never entirely involved in the world, in the sense of engaged absorption in daily life. This experience of disengagement, isolation, or ineffable distance from the world was accompanied by a tendency to observe or monitor his inner life. . . . "My first personal life is lost and is replaced by a third person perspective." To exemplify his predicament more concretely, he said that, for instance, listening to music on his stereo would give him an impression that the music somehow lacked its natural fullness, "as if something was wrong with the sound itself," and he tried to regulate the sound parameters on his stereo equipment, to no avail, and only to finally realise that he was somehow "internally watching" his own receptivity to music, his own mind receiving or registering of musical tunes. He, so to speak, witnessed his own sensory processes rather than living them. He experienced his own experiencing . . . and linked it to a long-lasting attitude of "adopting multiple perspectives," a tendency to regard any matter from all possible points of view. (pp. 124–125)

Sass and Parnas believe that it might be possible to predict the onset of psychosis from such accounts, charting the emergence and progression of schizophrenic symptoms. Is it possible to foresee a crisis and speak to a person about what she might encounter? Perhaps, but I am not sure.

I have written about this research on disturbance in ipseity at some length because it resonates with my experience of psychosis and my research for this book. A loss of selfhood maps on to a radical discontinuity of being and thought, losing coordinates of space and time, and finding new language that I have been tracing in first person accounts, in art and poetry and literary writing. Yet, as a Lacanian analyst, I question the proposal of "normal" (undisturbed) experiences of self as continuous and whole, and the very premise of such awareness of self without gaps. It is not in service of a fine theoretical point that I raise these matters. The problem with listening to psychosis from such premises is that we keep mistaking the perspectives of neurosis as the ground, the world-view that is normal, stable, and sane. But this conception of human experience, I believe, is mistaken.

Lacan has shown us that because we are born premature and subjected to the experience of voices, language, and demands of the Other from birth, the human body has been fractured into pieces, and reorganised in the Imaginary under the logic of signifiers from the start. It takes the neurotic years to discover this ground, to learn that his symptom was transmitted from his earliest life. And there is no unbroken awareness for us as humans: subjected to language, we are formed by it even in our pre-linguistic existence, including the emergence of words and thinking itself. The idea of self as bounded and continuous is tied to the ego, and the ego, through Lacan, becomes an illusion of wholeness made possible by the mirror stage, through which we become alienated from our actual, turbulent, and fractured bodily experience. In fact, we are split in our experience: conscious and unconscious. The self as a stable entity, moving through taken-for-granted tacit aspects of the world, is an Imaginary construction that the neurotic happens to believe is reality. What is Real is not connected to the self and its identifications; what is Real is the domain of the body, unknown, yet working to disrupt us all, psychotic or otherwise.

What we know, however, is that, in some respects, the psychotic has a distinctive experience. I argue it is different rather than disordered or deficient. The research by Sass and Parnas opens up new ways to enquire about the experience of psychosis and might point to its very emergence, provided we *do not mistake neurosis for normality*, for what is most basic to our humanity. Psychotic individuals might welcome a therapist who wonders about their experience of the body, thoughts, surroundings, including what has changed, what remains after psychosis. I applaud the idea of listening to nuanced alterations in a subjective sense of self, and to changes in perception, thought, the world itself. To ask about what comes to the foreground and what becomes tacit—both in a crisis and beyond psychosis—might teach us a great deal about the actual coordinates of that experience. Even more crucially, to ask about perception and experience invites the psychotic to speak, to know, to name what is most ineffable, so as not to be estranged entirely from the world and from others.

How the psychotic experiences her body might clarify aspects of psychosis and how it works. What happens when a strange experience of the body, self, and world veers into madness? Even more crucially, what works to stabilise the subject and halt the disorganisation of thought and speech? When invasive *jouissance* (the experience of the unbound drive in the body, intolerable and ineffable) is not contained or limited, it can lead to catastrophic disruption and disorganisation. To notice aspects of one's own body that seem suddenly alien, or to focus on points of self-experiencing rather than narrate the experience itself, could be attempts to find coherence. As such, these perceptions might function to stabilise someone at the edge of an abyss of disorganisation.

In a similar vein, a French psychiatrist, Abely (Declercq, 2004), noticed that sometimes the psychotic subject would become fixed on his image in the mirror just prior to developing a delusion. He called this phenomenon "the mirror sign". The subject recognises himself and wants to preserve that recognition. It is as though the subject seeks an image of sameness in the face of profoundly strange changes in his experience of the body. Declercq (2004) links the mirror sign to the real of the body, the eruption of *jouissance* in psychosis.

> If we read the observations concerning the mirror sign through Lacan's conceptualization of the real of the body, we could advance the hypothesis that the mirror sign indicates an eruption of jouissance. It may be the case that the subject is destabilized by an intrusion of jouissance in the body. Afterwards, the subjects in question are incapable of explaining what happened, except that something took place in their bodies. At the moment itself, they are perplexed and speechless. Lacan teaches us to recognise the real nature of the drive in this stupor or absence of signifiers. (p. 241)

We have seen, again and again, how the psychotic experiences the imposition of voices, perceptions, messages coming from outside herself, at exactly this place: "this stupor or absence of signifiers". If we take a step away from the disruption of language and re-making a new language to focus on the body and *jouissance*, it is possible to see a moment in which psychosis as madness may be triggered, *or avoided* via *another response*.

Within a recently developed Lacanian orientation, some individuals may be considered to have a psychotic structure even though there has been no psychotic break. The concept of "ordinary psychosis" was developed by Jacques-Alain Miller (2009) to describe a psychosis that has not been triggered, or has been triggered briefly and stabilised. This new turn offers a way of thinking about and treating patients who are not clearly neurotic, and do not present with any ongoing psychotic phenomena, but are assumed to be psychotic. A group of contemporary Lacanians have been engaged recently with questions about milder forms of psychosis that do not appear to fit into schizophrenia/paranoia classical paradigm. Their case presentations and discussions have signalled a re-engagement with Lacan's work on psychosis and an extension beyond his work. This new field relies on several of Lacan's concepts about psychosis: distinguishing between a triggered and untriggered psychosis, suppletion, and the sinthome. In brief, for a psychotic structure to be triggered into crisis, two conditions must be present: the structure of psychosis, and the foreclosed Name-of-the-Father must be called into opposition by some triggering event. Even when psychosis is triggered, the psychotic might find ways to stop the invasive *jouissance* and profound confusion that accompanies an encounter with a hole in the Symbolic as a result of the foreclosed signifier of the Name-of-the-Father. A suppletion is a stabilising substitute or a stand-in for what is missing in the Symbolic; it works to elide the Symbolic hole and avert a crisis. In the last years of his teaching, Lacan spoke of the development of a sinthome— knowing what to do with one's symptom. Miller's theorisation of ordinary psychosis makes use of these ideas with milder forms of psychosis, and offers us a way to reconsider the *body* in psychosis.

In his book, *Ordinary Psychosis and the Body: A Contemporary Lacanian Approach* (2014), Jonathan Redmond summarises the case of Adam, a young man who experiences transient psychotic symptoms. Redmond's case presentation is longer and more complex, but this extract captures a process of identification and symptom development that veers towards psychosis, and then away from it.

> During the course of his treatment, Adam's grandmother became seriously ill: on two occasions, she fell into a coma and the medical opinion was that she would not regain consciousness. Although she regained consciousness for several weeks after the first coma, life support was turned off on the second occasion. During both hospitalizations, Adam exhibited psychotic phenomena. During the first coma, Adam deteriorated rapidly in parallel with his grandmother: he became severely depressed, agitated and experienced racing thoughts – he said that he was going crazy and "wanted to be put out of his

misery". He reported fantasies of a drill going into his head and said he felt like a *machine* that was "out of order", a reference to the life support machine that was sustaining grandmother at the time. A triggering event produced negativism, racing thoughts, and extreme agitation. Adam recovered from these invasive phenomena shortly after grandmother regained consciousness. Several months later, grandmother fell into a second coma; her prognosis had deteriorated due to the discovery of systemic bone cancer and other complicating health factors relating to diabetes. Again, Adam experienced a triggering event; however, on this occasion hallucinatory elementary phenomena were evident, which suggested an escalation of psychosis. The emergence of an elementary phenomenon occurred at an important juncture – the family had decided to turn off life support and the burden of this difficult decision rested primarily with Adam's mother. As the family gathered around to turn off the life support machine, Adam "heard" his grandmother say that "she was scared and that she did not want to die". In subsequent weeks, an enigmatic experience connected to these hallucinatory elementary phenomena developed: Adam reported that his grandmother's talking pet bird, which he had inherited after her death, was trying to express new words to him. Here, the hallucinatory event that emerged at grandmother's death was displaced into the deciphering of the bird's vocalisations. However, no subsequent delusion or hallucinatory symptoms developed. For Adam, triggering events occurred in the context of mother's decision to end or prolong grandmother's life – these events appear to have triggered psychosis due to a confrontation with the Other's jouissance and the rupture of identification along the imaginary axis between Adam and grandmother. (pp. 49–50)

What resolves Adam's situation? Redmond tell us that Adam experiences painful leg cramps at night, which repeat an early trauma of having to wear braces to bed as a toddler, to correct a malformation. Redmond understands this symptom as a localisation of *jouissance* in the form of a bodily symptom that is outside the structure of neurosis, and functions as a form of stabilisation.

The field of ordinary psychosis raises many questions. How do we consider conversion symptoms that resist deciphering until the analysand is able to approach that work? And perversion is not neurosis, but also presents in the clinic with strange manifestations, especially enactments. Crucially, this new field offers way to orientate ourselves when the diagnosis is not clear, when we see transient symptoms that do not devolve into disorganised speech, delusion, or any recognisable form of madness. Yet, the patient suffers, reports unusual bodily experiences that will not decipher as neurotic symptoms, and commonly finds his own solution in the form of a new bodily symptom or ritual. Ordinary psychosis invites an enlarged understanding of the field of psychosis, considering how madness may be triggered or averted, experienced in milder forms and stabilised after a relatively short duration. This research asks us to reconsider not only what psychosis is, but also how the body (and its array of symptoms) are implicated, and to imagine possible trajectories in psychosis that we might not have seen in the clinic up to this point.

Ideas about suppletion and stabilisation have been part and parcel of considerations in the Lacanian clinic of psychosis for some time, even when the *diagnosis is clear*, that is, when someone has experienced a crisis or presents in the midst of one (see Fink, 2007). In fact, both Freud and Lacan understand delusion as a work of repair on the part of the psychotic, a repair that is stabilising. But what is teetering, so to speak, before that point?

But now I want to explore psychosis as a structure quite apart from madness, and return to the question of what psychosis is, at its heart. How can we consider psychosis in its own terms, beyond any implicit comparison to the "normality" of neurosis? The terms I explicate and develop below pertain to psychosis as *a structure without the advent of madness*—a structure that creates a new social link for humanity.

Working with Lacan's Seminar XXIII, *Joyce and the Sinthome* (1975–1976), I want to highlight four points of orientation in the psychotic structure: (1) the ego ruptures into an open form that divests itself of the body and its affects; (2) the ego has enigmatic functions; it *is* the unconscious, and the unconscious becomes accessible through "the error" of epiphany; (3) when *jouissance* invades the entire body, it disorganises the subject and brings him close to the void, and this problematic must be treated by the psychotic himself; (4) the sinthome, illustrated through the typology of a Borromean knot, becomes a know-how with one's symptom. The sinthome also creates a singular *jouissance* and a new social link.

First, I shall unravel these four points through Lacan in the last lesson of Seminar XXIII, and then provide an exegesis of how they work in various writings by Joyce. In this 1975–1976 seminar, Lacan creates a new topology to describe the psychotic structure, showing us how a fourth term added to the Borromean knot of *Real, Symbolic, and Imaginary* allows the subject to cohere, when any of three orders might have become disconnected. I will not go into the details; that is beyond the scope of what I want to say here. However, throughout this seminar, and especially towards the end of Seminar XXIII, Lacan describes characteristics of the psychotic structure that are striking in their implication for how we think of psychosis and its possibilities.

Lacan speculates that in the psychotic structure the ego is not the form of a circle, but has opened itself to the Real. The open form of the ego is far from a liability. It is a form that veers from the illusion of a bounded whole firmly connected to a body image. Lacan tells us that Joyce can detach from his body, "to be shed, like the skin of a fruit" (XI, p. 10) and he has a body "like a piece of furniture" (XI, p. 16). The self, body, and ego are not unified; in fact, the body slips this purely Imaginary unity and frees itself of the Imaginary; the ego is open to the Real and remains open. The open ego, with access to the Real, has an enigmatic function. In this function, Lacan tells us, the ego *is* the unconscious. Lacan takes a step away from the unconscious as structured by signifiers (of the Symbolic), and declares, "One thinks against a signifier. . . . One leans against a signifier in order to think" (XI, p. 18).

How does Joyce think? He thinks through encounters with his errors. Lacan argues that for Joyce "epiphanies are all always characterised by the same thing: an error" and "the unconscious is linked to the Real, thanks to the mistake" (XI, p. 17). The psychotic leans into this problem with language: he finds enigmas, and his unconscious produces epiphanies, which, in turn, read as indecipherable. The psychotic also has the problematic that *jouissance* invades the entire body, disorganises the subject, and brings him close to the void, and this problematic must be treated by the psychotic himself. Joyce discovers how to take language apart and build it as "lalangue" (Lacan, 1989), a polyphony of resonances that treat *jouissance* as melody, and raise the detritus of sounds to the level of art. Joyce creates work meant to keep scholars busy with his enigma for a very long time. In this way, he makes his name. Here, we come full circle with the title of Lacan's seminar; the sinthome is a solution that introduces a singular *jouissance* into a social link.

If we listen in, as it were, to the rupture of the open ego, what we hear and see is something very peculiar. In the following extract, an argument breaks out between Stephen, the protagonist in *Portrait of the Artist as a Young Man* (2005[1914]), and his peers, over the question of who is the greatest poet, leading to a physical encounter and its aftermath:

> — And who do you think is the greatest poet? asked Boland, nudging his neighbour.
>
> — Byron, of course, answered Stephen.
>
> Heron gave the lead and all three joined in a scornful laugh.
>
> — What are you laughing at? asked Stephen.
>
> — You, said Heron. Byron the greatest poet! He's only a poet for uneducated people.
>
> — He must be a fine poet! said Boland.
>
> — You may keep your mouth shut, said Stephen, turning on him boldly . . .
>
> — Here, catch hold of this heretic, Heron called out. In a moment Stephen was a prisoner.
>
> — Tate made you buck up the other day, Heron went on, about the heresy in your essay.
>
> — I'll tell him tomorrow, said Boland.
>
> — Will you? said Stephen. You'd be afraid to open your lips.
>
> — Afraid?
>
> — Ay. Afraid of your life.
>
> — Behave yourself! cried Heron, cutting at Stephen's legs with his cane.
>
> It was the signal for their onset. Nash pinioned his arms behind while Boland seized a long cabbage stump, which was lying in the gutter. Struggling and kicking under the cuts of the cane and the blows of the knotty stump Stephen was borne back against a barbed wire fence.
>
> — Admit that Byron was no good.
>
> — No.
>
> — Admit.
>
> — No . . .

At last after a fury of plunges he wrenched himself free. His tormentors set off towards Jones's Road, laughing and jeering at him, while he, half blinded with tears, stumbled on, clenching his fists madly and sobbing.

While he was still repeating the Confiteor amid the indulgent laughter of his hearers and while the scenes of that malignant episode were still passing sharply and swiftly before his mind he wondered why he bore no malice now to those who had tormented him. He had not forgotten a whit of their cowardice and cruelty but the memory of it called forth no anger from him. All the descriptions of fierce love and hatred which he had met in books had seemed to him therefore unreal. Even that night as he stumbled homewards along Jones's Road he had felt that some power was divesting him of that sudden-woven anger as easily as a fruit is divested of its soft ripe peel. (pp. 91–93)

Stephen does not dissociate from his body in this incident with his peers, and neither does he repress the details of the beating. But he is at a distance from his body, none the less. Elsewhere in the novel, he speaks to his fingers, hurrying them through buttoning his coat, as though they are not part of him. Here, he sheds "that sudden-woven anger" in his body, and expresses disbelief in "fierce love and hatred". The open ego does not attach to affects; no more does it flee the experience itself. The body and its affects are simply detachable, woven, and shed, and, therefore, foreign to the ego. Joyce must know this experience to create it in the character of Stephen.

There is much more I might say about this phenomenon in Joyce. However, here I just want to illustrate the open ego, and the idea that the ego has enigmatic functions; it *is* the unconscious, accessible through "the error" of epiphany. From the time Joyce wrote *Dubliners* (2000[1914]), he created moments of profound confusion in his characters, individuals caught in enigmas and riddles, and alongside the enigmas we find "epiphanies", written in vivid, almost hallucinatory fragments. Joyce did not present epiphanies as spiritual revelations, or realisations, but as moments portrayed outside of conscious knowledge.

Lacan reads such epiphanies as instances of radical foreclosure of meaning, in which the Real, the impossible to say, to know, or to realise, emerges. Joyce makes use of these moments of profound dislocation or confusion, and has done so from the start of his writing life. For example, in *Dubliners*, he uses indirect discourse (a point of view that allows his readers a broader view than the protagonist narrating the story), to show his characters are mistaken about the whole picture. Often, we also find momentary, vivid impressions that the characters cannot explain or even fully formulate. In this sense, Joyce's epiphanies are inextricably connected to enigmas. Joyce raised the two-sided experience of enigma and epiphany to an art in his writing. In his biography of Joyce, Richard Ellman (1983[1959]) documented some things Joyce said and raised them to the level of nearly mythic quotes: "A man's errors are volitional and are his portals of discovery" (p. 646), and "I've put in so many enigmas and puzzles that it will keep the professors busy for centuries arguing over what I meant, and that's the only way of insuring one's immortality" (p. 573). The latter is Joyce's famous reply to a request for a plan of *Ulysses*.

What, we might well ask, is this link between the enigma–epiphany pairing in Joyce and his repeated construction of a riddle, of himself at the heart of a riddle, when reading his work? This turns out to be an important link, in my view, because the answer to a riddle is a work of construction. I return to lesson four in Seminar XXIII, where Lacan reminds us of a riddle posed by Stephen in *Ulysses* as a young schoolmaster to his students: "The cock crew / the sky was blue; / the bells in heaven / were striking eleven. / 'tis time for this poor soul / to go to heaven" (Lacan, IV, p. 14). The class cannot figure it out, and Stephen provides the answer, "The fox burying his grandmother under the bush" (Lacan, IV, p. 14). Of course, this does not make "sense". But Lacan calls the answer "a creation", and also claims that analysis has this kind of resonance; "it is a response to a riddle". He goes on to point out that "analysis is a matter of splicing and sutur-ing" (Lacan, IV, p. 15). What is at stake is enjoyment, and to render that freedom of enjoyment possible (recall that enjoyment, by this point in Lacan's teaching, refers to the *body* enjoying),

> When we make this splice . . . we teach him [analysand] to splice, to make a splice between his sinthome and this parasitic Real of enjoy-ment. And what is characteristic of our operation, to render this enjoy-ment possible, is the same thing as what I will write: j'ouis-sens. It is the same thing as to hear a meaning. (Lacan, IV, p 15)

To slow this down a bit, what Lacan proposes here is that analysis follow the path of the sinthome, which is a construction. We have moved very quickly from the enigma and epiphany to the construction of a riddle, and from the riddle to the necessity to re-situate enjoyment by taking language apart and putting it together again. This, in short, is what Joyce does in his art.

In Seminar XXIII, Lacan shows us that language can be rewritten, broken, and dislocated, to the point that Joyce finishes by dissolving language itself. In short, Joyce's solution, from his creation of enigmas and epiphanies in *Dubliners* to the unreadable lines on every page of *Finnegans Wake* (1999[1939]), is to refashion language, destroying it and remaking it, so that the entire Symbolic order becomes filled with Joyce's private *jouissance*. In doing so, Joyce makes a new social link of Joyceans, those of us who are devoted to unravelling his riddles because the resonance of his language makes language new. The sinthome might be tied to a private *jouissance*, but it speaks to a wider social link, and, more accurately, it creates a new social link that did not exist before.

These, then, are the coordinates of a life structured by psychosis and lived outside madness: an open ego, the unconscious as a function of the ego through enigma and epiphany, and the transformation of an invasive, disorganising *jouissance* into a new construction, the sinthome. For the psychotic structure, incandescent alphabets carry the *jouissance* of the subject, and when they are used to make a new social link, we see a construction that is *not delusion*. Incandescent alphabets also reference the idiosyncratically encoded, indecipherable language and images of Prinzhorn's art collection, which become part of delusion, closed to questioning. What I want to emphasise here is that incandescent alphabets can be transformed or configured as a sinthome.

What is more, the path of the sinthome that Lacan describes is also the trajectory of analysis in the last years of Lacan's teaching. The splice that makes a new link between the analysand's symptom and the parasitic Real of enjoyment in language, *j'ouis-sens*, pertains to the psychoanalytic clinic. As analysts, we would do well to listen for nonsense and melody, and this is the case not only for the psychotic, but for *everyone* who would do an analysis after Lacan.

This chapter covers a wide range of ways to listen to psychosis, to consider the experience itself in all its heterogeneity, and to respond to psychosis in its own terms. In psychosis, the individual considers the great enigma to which he is being subjected. This draws him into a network of ideas. The strangest aspects of his speech might be evidence that the psychotic is working to repair what has gone awry in language, in time, in order, and in the universe or the cosmos. This is a work of restoration and construction. Beyond (and sometimes before) a triggered crisis, psychosis may be stabilised through a suppletion, such as a bodily symptom that limits invasive *jouissance*, or a relationship that anchors the individual in her life. It is also possible to live in a psychotic structure without the advent into a crisis or madness in any recognisable form.

*   *   *

The experiments with language made by Joyce deserve our attention and elaboration beyond the Seminars of Lacan. *The Buffalo Notebooks* (Joyce, 2003) document the evolution of *Finnegans Wake*, a work in progress over a period of seventeen years, and are an extraordinary resource, not only for scholars of literature, but for psychoanalysts interested in incandescent alphabets in the making.

Jonathan McCreedy, in "Everyword for oneself but Code for us all! The shapes of sigla in Finnegans Wake" (2010), highlights the shapes Joyce created while working on *Finnegans Wake*:

> In short, the sigla are a collection of symbols or pictorials which Joyce composed for use in his *Finnegans Wake* notebooks. Each character: HCE, ALP, Shaun, Shem, Issy etc. has a sigla, which would represent their name in shorthand. Joyce detailed his basic sigla system to Harriet Shaw Weaver, in a March 1924 letter. The eight protagonists are listed here in their purest forms:
>
> ⊓ (Earwicker, HCE by moving letter around)
>
> △ Anna Livia Plurabelle
>
> ⊏ Shem
>
> ∧ Shaun
>
> S Snake
>
> P S.Patrick
>
> T Tristan
>
> ⊥ Isolde
>
> ✕ Mamalujo
>
> ☐ This stands for the [novel's] title but I do not wish to say it yet until the book has written more of itself.

What strikes me (although I am not a Joyce scholar and do not know the genetic research on Joyce), is that this series of shapes (that accompany the names of the characters of *Finnegans Wake*) read as a code, but do not function as code. Instead, the shapes explode into new language that changes how we hear language. But, initially, these sigla appear to me not unlike the incandescent alphabets of the artists in Chapter Four. What is the difference? Joyce uses the sigla to hold a place for what will come (for example, the title, not yet formulated). The novel he writes is not as a closed system. And, in so far as scholars study the sigla and their relation to Joyce's writing in progress, they form a specialised social link among Joyce scholars.

I might go on and on, drop down the deep rabbit hole of the Notebooks, to see what I might find, and better, hear, the *j'ouis-sens* of *Finnegans Wake* unfolding. It could be another project for another time. However, for now, I am reminded that incandescent alphabets (language stitched to the Real that writes itself and does not stop) arise out of silence at the edge of a void.

> I'll stop, I'll end, it's the end already, but I must go on, without anyone, without anything but me, but my voice, that is to say I'll stop, I'll end, it's the end already, short-lived, what is it, a little hole, you go down into it, into the silence . . . someone calls me, I crawl out again, what is it, a little hole, in the wilderness. . . .
>
> You must go on.
>
> I can't go on.
>
> I'll go on. (Beckett, 1994[1951], p. 151)

This extract speaks back to the trajectory of this chapter, from speech with an elusive address that is difficult to follow, to the stakes of our listening to psychosis in its diverse moments and manifestations, to the creation of new language that does not stop writing itself at the place of a true hole.

A true hole—outside meaning, outside the chain of signifiers, and outside discourse—leaves in its wake a river of Real *jouissance* that runs through our bodies, collecting the melodies of the river, all those sounds we heard before we had language. The psychotic knows this, lives this experience of language, and sometimes makes use of it.

CHAPTER EIGHT

Psychoanalysis remade: a way through psychosis

"Soul / take thy risk"

(Emily Dickinson, Amherst Manuscript # 357)

F reud realised that the classic form of psychoanalysis invented for neurosis, which depended on deciphering symptoms, would not work readily with psychosis because psychotics did not present symptoms to be analysed. However, he questioned his own contraindication of psychoanalysis with psychotics: "By suitable changes to the method [of psychoanalysis] we may succeed in overcoming this contraindication [against analysis]- and so be able to initiate a psychotherapy of the psychoses" (Freud, 1904a, p. 253). Rare analysts, such as Frieda Fromm-Reichmann and Harold Searles, followed Freud's advice and did just that in the middle decades of the twentieth century, and they were remarkably successful in their treatment of psychosis. In contemporary time, however, psychoanalysis is rarely considered as a feasible way of working with psychosis. Short hospital stays and aggressive medication of symptoms have become the norm.

179

How might psychoanalysis be re-created for psychosis in our time? This question arises in relation to Freud's contraindication—*what is it* in psychosis that will *not yield* to deciphering? While this question is important, not *everything* the psychotic says and believes lies beyond the realm of what he can decipher. In fact, when psycho-analysis is conceived as a creative construction for what has been impossible to know, impossible to name, then an analytic experience offers a particular premise for work with psychosis. While the analytic work on the side of the analyst is ethical, responding to each patient as a unique case, the *creative construction of the analysis* is up to the analysand. This is important because a paranoid transference can evolve as the trapped subject of the analyst's construction confronts the omnipotent and omniscient Other. The premise is that analysis is an ethical practice that facilitates creative work; it is, most radically, "a raid on the inarticulate" (Eliot, 1940, p. 5) that changes lives. This is the case for anyone who embarks on analysis with an analyst who does not get in the way with his own symptom, but it is especially crucial, I think, with psychosis.

I interviewed two colleagues working in different psychoanalytic traditions, sending them questions as a guide to our conversation before we met. My questions encompassed psychoanalytic listening, the position of the analyst, transference, and how to accompany patients who were disorganised through a psychotic crisis. I did not follow any interview sequence, but followed the logic and priorities of my two colleagues. I chose these two because they each have created a form of psychoanalysis that enables life-changing work with psychotic patients and I wanted to hear about that work, the ideas that formed it in the past, and the questions and ideas that guide it now.

* * *

I met Barri Belnap at Austen Riggs. She was one of several senior staff who joined a Lacanian seminar on psychosis I offered to residents and interns. She also participated in a year-long exploration of Lacan's *Seminar XXIII* offered through the Lacanian School of San Francisco in a group that met monthly at Hampshire College in Amherst, Massa-chusetts. In both these contexts I was struck by her curiosity, her keen clinical commentaries, and the richness of her experience with psy-chosis. She is a psychiatrist on staff at the Austen Riggs Center in Stockbridge, Massachusetts. There she offers psychoanalytic psychotherapy to patients, including psychotic patients, four days a week. Patients stay in residence for six weeks up to several years, depending on their case. It is long enough to make real changes in their lives. Dr Belnap's clinical investigations focus on understanding how symptoms address themselves to current developmental needs in a family context. She has written on the intergenerational transmission of trauma, and an approach to the treatment of first break psychosis in adolescents and their families. She also works in private practice and at Providence Hospital in Western Massachusetts as a doctor on call. When I met Barri for her interview, it was as though she had absorbed my questions and tucked them into nested clinical stories. In our interview, I remembered my own questions in moments at the interstices of her working theory and something beyond language in her clinical work. I had the impression of nests made from gathered sticks, straw and blown bits, intricate nests she had already made with her young patients and was now bringing to me. Barri began with a framing of psychoanalytic listening and a story about working with a young psychotic patient and his family.

"Psychoanalytic listening believes a mind is making sense and is learning to use itself even within the disorganisation of acute psychosis. The listening position of the psychoanalyst becomes the way the patient listens to his or her own mind. 'What do I observe my mind doing; what hypotheses can I derive from these observed patterns and from the experience of my mind; and how do I test the truth, value, and relevance of these hypotheses in relation to this particular context I find myself in at present?' Psychoanalysis provides a structure for listening to psychosis without the pressure to understand it. It puts the analyst in a position to join the patient with a curiosity about mind and experience that is respectful."

"I can see that. Can you say more about this particular version of psychoanalysis?"

"Some analytic practices ask what or who caused the psychosis, often raising concerns about the mother's relation to the child or the absence of the paternal metaphor. I don't ask where psychosis begins. That question is unanswerable. It doesn't help. Many parents also seem to be looking for the answer to that question. When I am working with a patient and his or her family, particularly when the first break occurs during adolescence, I am not looking for what parents did wrong or to hypothesise how parents made their child sick.

Instead I focus on how the parents have tried to find a position from which to be a parent. I listen for the developmental question facing the patient and his family, where they look for resources, and what is in the way of the unfolding developmental process."

"How do you work with these questions in your practice?" I ask.

"I want to understand the edge of learning about the current developmental priorities of the parents and the patient. These are different roles and I listen for how the dilemmas around a particular developmental impasse are uniquely defined in relation to each. For example, the mother will relate to her child as a mother, as part of a parental pair (the mother and father together) and as the 'other than mother' aspect of her identity. The father will occupy similar roles. The patient is in the role of an adolescent child of his parents and also making steps to take up the role of an adult child of his parents, at the same time he or she is beginning to claim membership in groups outside of the family. His actions and speech function in the service of these various roles."

"Can you give an example of your work with a family?" I ask.

"In families, conflict can focus on who defines reality; this is worse when a family member is identified with having, or having had, a psychotic experience. Usually, the patient is assumed to be unable to 'reality test'. In one clinical situation, a delusional young man believed he was destined to be the king after the apocalypse, Jesus, or the devil. His psychosis also evidenced itself by odd verbal references, somatic symptoms, and disorganised speech and behaviour. His mother made great efforts to reach him through identifying how he was in exactly the position she had to her father. The patient would speak back in a rage, 'No. To you I am like footsteps in the sand that you fill with water', or, alternatively, 'You cut my words like the queen of swords.' He was protesting being put in the same position as his mother. He needed a position from which he could be similar but not exactly the same, because without that he could not feel his agency. In such situations, the communication between mother and son takes place in whatever ways they can find. This mother fought to give her children a better life than she had with her own parents. Her success as a mother seemed to depend on accomplishing this goal. She tried to help her son be a different kind of man than those who had failed her miserably in the past. She had a wish to reverse a problem she faced in her childhood and was trying to interrupt the transmission of a generational pattern. She wanted to create in her son a "new other", a utopian solution in which he was to become a different kind of man. Her motherhood was devoted to this aim."

"You, and they, came to see this in the family work?"

"In a family meeting, a link presented itself between his delusion of being the king after the apocalypse and the family process. This link included the embodiment in his delusion of his mother's deeply felt wishes for his future—that is, as an agent of transformation of a catastrophic situation. In the meeting, the boy and his mother were fighting over their different views of the reality of something that had happened. He spoke of his fear that her reaction to his saying what he felt would be 'apocalyptic'. From the role of therapist, I noticed the use of this word and wondered out loud if there might be a link between the apocalypse of the delusion and this moment in the meeting. If he injured his mother, the effect seemed apocalyptic. In a parallel fashion, his delusion was that after the apocalypse he would become a utopian figure who would be able to save people and create a new world. This was similar to the utopian ambitions evident in the way his mother took up her maternal role—that is, in her hope to raise him to be a better and different kind of man."

"There is something very real that the psychotic carries in the family?" I ask.

"Yes, I see psychosis as containing a kind of expert knowledge that I can try to learn something about. This is a foundational principle I have in mind when I am sitting with a psychotic patient. My goal is not to get rid of symptoms. Symptoms say something that can't be said any other way in the moment and context of role relationships that create them. Psychoanalytic listening provides a structured context that supports the thinking through and practising of these transformational steps."

"And your own position as you work through a process of transformation?"

"In the first stages of treatment, I try to discover each parent's theory of emotion and mind. I want to understand the model they use to define their own experience and that of their child. To do this, I might meet with parents and a family co-therapist weekly. Sometimes, the patient is present, but usually the patient prefers not to be. I might ask what they think their child is dealing with. You always learn things from the parents that the patient cannot tell you. Parents need a space to be able to learn and question how to be parents. This is a parallel piece of work to that which is going on in the psychotherapeutic work with the patient. In both the individual therapy and in the family work, the position of analytic listening works at the relationship between roles and how they develop their mind's capacity to use reason in relation to their current context. By working at this juncture, I am working at what sustains or disrupts the social link that is theorised to be so important in the treatment of psychosis."

"Yes," I say, "This is very respectful of the parents, and yet I wonder how you respond when you are thrust into the role of the expert—as analyst or as a psychiatrist?"

"When psychoanalysts or other therapists assume that they know better than the patient or parents, they stop listening. It is a disaster. Those presuming to know what is best for the patient become a "crazy" example of a delusion, but this time on the side of the therapist who presumes to know more than he can know. The patient or family member must defer their efforts to come to know what is true and instead identify with the authority claims of "medical science" or the practitioner. I think it is important when providing information to families about ideas promoted by medical science that it be done without making claims of absolute authority. This can easily be done by stating that medical science at this time believes X or Y. Whether or not those findings can be generalised to the family must be tested by the family. *Their* experience will be the judge."

"In your work with patients in psychosis, and especially in the transference, what are the edges where you might be baffled or frustrated?"

"There are two times. One is when the patient has started to come out of psychosis and the other is when I am trying to appreciate psychotic anxiety without trying to change it. From the position of the therapist, the experience of psychotic anxiety creates a strong impulse to know and to change things. To resist the impulse is challenging. It is difficult to be made aware of the potential senselessness that the experience of psychosis sometimes communicates. To feel crazy in a relationship where one is assumed to be making no sense is common enough; it is familiar to someone who has never been psychotic. This form of anxiety may be hidden by an obstinate certainty and concreteness. I also find difficulty occurs at the stage of recovery from psychosis in which the patient is aware that he has lost the ability to be in, or control going into, the delusion. Patients will say they wish they could be crazy or psychotic again because of the pain and dread they experience at anticipating what it will take to join the world without the delusion/psychosis. I find I struggle emotionally with the wish to forget the struggles that I experienced with the patient during the months or years of listening respectfully to the experiences brought to the surface by the psychosis."

"Can you give a clinical example of anxiety on the side of the psychotic?"

"In the context of an ongoing treatment of first break psychosis, I was called to see a patient as the doctor on call because he developed a new delusion that aliens were going to track him because he had a chip in his head. He was struggling with the wish to take a knife to his head to cut out this alienating device (alienating because it made him different from other people). I asked him why he developed this concern on that particular day and he recalled that this was the day his friends were graduating from college. He said he felt alienated from them and the life he had been anticipating leading. This led to a conversation about his lost dreams. He then spoke of preferring to be psychotic again and I could understand that because of the depth of his feelings."

"Are there other situations you struggle with in relation to the treatment of psychosis?"

"It is difficult when hospital staff become afraid of a patient in a psychotic state. Their efforts to reduce him to an 'it' is painful. Behaviours that might affect any of us seem exaggerated to staff when they suspect psychosis. Psychotic patients are at times trying to understand a human experience that envelops all of us but which we don't think about much, such as the difference between what happens and what is said about what happens. Their efforts to find a way to communicate what they sense but don't have words for yet can be disconcerting. At times, they question cherished truths and illusions that are consensually agreed upon by staff. So much of the world speaks in ways that are not truthful. There is integrity, I believe, in the researching efforts of psychotic individuals to ferret out the truth from the deception. The effort to know the truth might be in conflict with the need to test out if others also are invested in the truth or some illusion. The patient will face situations that seem to demand that truth be sacrificed for a relationship. This dynamic can cause a lot of conflict between staff in an inpatient or residential treatment setting. If you think of how paranoia functions between people, it generates information about who and what to trust."

"I wonder if you can speak to disorganisation in psychosis, which can sometimes precipitate a crisis, sometimes indicates someone is in crisis, and sometimes is just a passing state, but expresses itself in certain ways, including disorganised speech. How do you accompany someone into that and through it?"

"There is something too difficult to put into words. The process of marking the meaning of experience between therapist and patient may not happen with words at that stage. Words might have been experienced as untrustworthy and may be used as objects or decoys to test the desire of the therapist. Experience from the past and from contexts other than the time spent with the patient in therapy is usually not usable as a referent point. It is not possible to assume a similarity of experience in realms of disorganisation. The basis for later therapeutic work is created in the sessions by the events and the therapist's memory of events that occur between patient and therapist. The narrative history of those events begins to create a social link and place both the patient and therapist in a socio-psycho-historical chain that neither controls completely."

"And before that, when narration is next to impossible?" I ask.

"In a state of disorganisation, the patient could be in touch with experiences that he does not have a way to communicate with words or images. Action communication is prominent. The patient might experience words as not trustworthy. They might come to him as if from nowhere, as he has trouble identifying the role he is in and that others are speaking from. He might be testing the therapist's desire to know his experience *vs.* some other perverse use of the therapist–patient relationship that caters instead to the therapist's narcissistic desire. One patient, at an early stage of his treatment, was very disorganised. The objects he made in his shop became the markings of a perception of experience that, over time, became the basis for our making sense of things. He had at that stage not divulged his delusions, but he looked like Jesus. He fashioned a heavy cross and wore it around his neck. Going through the details of his day, he would tell me what he made. He began making rings. He wore them and soon other patients began asking him to make some for them. The rings then took on the status of a gift. At a certain point in the treatment he reflected on the cross and said that he had felt afraid that he would float away and that the wooden cross held him to the earth. The rings made the cross less important. I wondered out loud if the rings became a gift that meant something to people he cared about so that the gifts connected him to others and the earth, making the cross less necessary. I invited him to consider it a crazy idea if it did not make sense to him, as I held his sense of things to be more important than my idea. Sometimes the psychotic person cannot find the right words."

"And those who are seeking a way to speak truth just won't settle for the approximate!" I say, and we both laugh.

"Regardless of the patient's disorganisation, I hold the belief that, as people, we all face certain *human* dilemmas. What differentiates us is where we look for the resources to answer and address those dilemmas. I respect that another person's mind is one that I cannot know, but I can assume that minds are always making meaning. My interest and curiosity in the sense my patient is making grounds both of us. Psychoanalytic curiosity, in its respect for the other and the refusal to narcissistically use/enjoy the patient, was a gift to me that I give to my patients. This gift says 'you are someone of value and interest.' Even a person in a disorganised state feels recognised when met that way. This meeting creates an early social link."

"The meaning the person is trying to make infiltrates all your work even when she or he is disorganised in speaking or unable to speak?"

"In psychosis, I believe the question 'how do I know what I know' is the priority. The corollary is 'how do you know what you know?' The patient is investigating the process of answering both lines of questioning. This will become the basis for having his own experience from which he can judge the truth claims of others. Leston Havens was my residency director and he encouraged us to take a position *side by side* with the patient, both of us metaphorically, and sometimes actually, looking out a window together on to the world."

If these might be considered nested stories (and for me they are nested in delicate, daring moments), they transmit something of Barri's impulse to seek out the truths of psychosis, while offering a language, names for what she hears, things her patients might make use of, to re-read and re-charge their own speech, their own creative efforts to make a new social link. Barrie's theory is not my theory, and yet her language conveys a deep respect for what is human in psychosis. It is a crackly, static language with its own energy; and it answers something in me.

*   *   *

I came into contact with Charles Turk first as a colleague attending Lacanian seminars offered by GIFRIC (Groupe interdisciplinaire freudien de recherche et d'intervention clinique et culturelle) in Quebec City, Canada. After years of working together in the summer seminars, we began to write letters to one another about our lives, experiences, and interests. When I first knew him, my impression was that he spoke in tangents and circles, and seldom got to the point. It took me a few years to see that his mode of speech bore traces of his thoughts unfolding, something most people have learnt to cover over. I saw that he listened with a far-away look that gathered everything into a fine net. And I learnt that he liked to walk city streets on a diagonal simply because it was more efficient to do so. He would explain, "It is a matter of following the hypotenuse of a right triangle—if A, B, and C define the points of the triangle, then going from A to C is quicker." Later still (and only through my own research), I learned that Charles Turk received an exemplary psychiatrist award from NAMI (National Alliance on Mental Illness) for his work with severely ill patients in a public partial hospitalisation programme. He did his psychoanalytic training at the Center for Psychoanalytic Study, Chicago, and has since joined the faculty of the Chicago Center for Psychoanalysis, where he now works as a mentor to the next generation. He is a founding member of the Chicago Circle of the Ecole Freudienne du Quebec, and recently has been asked to join the Clinical Direction of that School as a representative of the several Circles that now exist in the USA. I count him as a friend, someone I do not always agree with, but one who is remarkably and entirely himself, while also being an analyst who works with lost cases and refuses to give up on patients others would not even consider taking on.

Charles begins, "Your questions are formidable—they seem beyond me." Yet, as he begins to speak about his life and experience treating psychosis, Charles circles around his own speech, as if what he does as an analyst looks back at him from an odd angle. He is incredulous, blinking at me, when he tells me about patients getting better. Listening to him, I am reminded of the grey feathers on the backs of ostriches. They look quite ordinary, but little golden chicks are hidden there, hiding without subterfuge. You must know they are there to even bother to look for them. Otherwise, nothing is there, nothing of note, certainly nothing alive. Charles circles a memory of childhood, the impetus to become a psychiatrist and an analyst, and his long-term engagement with the Freudian School of Quebec and the GIFRIC seminars.

"One of my very early memories—certainly before the age of three—was of playing on the sunlit floor and glancing up to see my parents smiling at me. Caught in a beam of sunlight, they were beaming at me. In due course my personal quest, my problem, became just what I could beam back at them. Freud noted that the analyst can take the analysand no further than the frontier where his own analysis had found its limit. It is an ethical question. I have been subject to a set of experiences that created 'an infernal pit'. I might describe its sides as composed of my ego, failing in its pursuit of my ideal ego, a shabby 'medical' offering to the eternally unsatisfied ghosts of my parents who reside in the core of my superego. Gradually, not without some pain, I have given up on this quest and have gravitated—not without trepidation—towards an 'ethical practice'. So, I might conclude that the fruits of my own analysis have enabled me to make use of these experiences, without succumbing to them. And so the question that I keep posing to myself in my work is, 'What I am moved to say—does it arise from my symptom or from my desire to know?' This question of ethics and my take on my own 'infernal pit' are derived from my years of study within the EFQ (Freudian School of Quebec) and GIFRIC."

I ask Charles about his early work with psychosis, what it was like in the beginning.

He begins with a memory of his first supervisor. "I have cultivated the memory of this supervisor, whom I call 'my nemesis', in recognition of the importance of preserving the figure of an ideal persecutor. Now, this particular supervisor also conducted a clinical case seminar where I had occasion to present a case that troubled me a great deal. The case was that of a sixteen-year-old developmentally disabled, schizophrenic patient who was withdrawn and mute. My report of my meeting with this adolescent went something like this: we entered the consulting room (I might add that this was a very small room among a warren of little rooms that connotes something labyrinthine in nature). I asked him how he was. He sat silently for about a minute, rose, left, and entered another room. I followed him, said that I realised he might be uncomfortable in my presence, but that as he was in the hospital it was important that he speak to me about himself. He did not respond, again rose and left. I kept following.

At last my supervisor could bear it no longer. He slammed his hand down upon the table and exclaimed, 'I don't know how you can stand to see this kind of patient!' That declaration was my 'emancipation proclamation'. My nemesis, the supervising analyst that I hated, provided me with something necessary in this context. It's good to have a foil when you are young; it makes you take a stance. And now I would expand upon that to explain why I nurture an image of this man, whom I never have occasion to see. One confronts the labyrinth of one's unconscious and, like Theseus in search of the Minotaur, when you have the living breathing monster to grapple with, your uncertainty vanishes; you know what you are up against: my nemesis, better than my nightmare."

"Can you go back to when you first started to practise?" I ask. "How did you work then?"

Charles begins again. "When I first started private practice, I had a patient who kept having brief catatonic episodes. When I first met her, she was seated on the floor of a quiet room, legs spread apart, rhythmically smashing herself in her face with both fists, as she cried out, 'Rats—rats.' I would later discover that she was convinced that she was splitting apart and radioactive garbage spilled from her body to be consumed by a swarm of rats. When her psychiatrist left the Chicago area, he referred her to me. She had been hospitalised four times in the previous two years. I was determined that she wouldn't return there, and this never happened during the forty years we worked together."

"Tell me about that work with her," I say.

He smiles, "You know sometimes we are the last to know. One day she said to me, 'One of my students . . .' in passing. I asked, 'What students?' 'Oh—I didn't tell you—I've begun giving piano lessons to children.' It turned out that all the mothers in the neighbourhood were beating a path to her door, so effective an instructor she was. Once, she described how a child snuggled up against her during a lesson. This pleased her. This from a woman who had been convinced she was filled with radioactive garbage.

"She would try to rid herself of this stuff by raking her wrists with her fingernails until they bled. She would then bandage her wrists. Once, while lying on the couch, she raised up her bare wrists. 'Look,' she said, 'no marks.' You may wonder why, contrary to all recommendations and to common sense, I would have a psychotic person lie on the couch. It was purely pragmatic. On the couch she did not risk looking at me, 'to find that I did not exist' as she told me, and perhaps to avoid exposing me to her lethal gaze, I conjecture. Once, after emerging from a catatonic episode, she gazed at me straight on. Weeks later she asked, 'Dr T—do you have a moustache?'"

I smile at this; as long as I have known him, Charles has had a moustache. I wonder aloud, "And when a person can't organise himself to speak, what does your part look like?"

Charles replies, "Often it looks like nothing at all. But I'll follow any lead. For example, with this patient I often had to literally hold her. As we sat next to each other on the floor, I'd insist that she tell me what had just happened. One day, in speechless frustration, she raised her hand and gestured as if she were using a pencil. I provided pen and paper and for the next several months she made crude drawings of her head being split open by lightening bolts and we were able to engage in much discussion about the ramifications of this. I suppose this is an example of scrabbling about to use what you have at hand in the spur of the moment. In contrast to her crude sketches, she was, in fact, a talented artist, as revealed by booklets of photos of her work she would later bring to me."

Charles pauses and adds, "One day after this she responded to another of my queries as to what had just happened by saying, 'I am in a pit and you always put a ladder down into it and so I can climb out.'"

I say to Charles, "Some of our colleagues think that psychotics can't use metaphor, you know." We both laugh heartily about that.

Then he becomes serious, "The thing about the pit is that it's not foreign to me."

I ask, "How was it that you reinvented a form of psychoanalysis that might work?"

Incredulous that he might have done exactly this, Charles replies, "Oh, I'd often say to myself, I'll just throw in the towel! It's useless. There's nothing anyone can do. I'd listen to myself, and retreat from 'doing' something, but persist in meeting with the patient. I was looking for *anything* that would counter 'it's hopeless', anything that would open up a space for the work."

"And, are you still seeing her? What is she like now?" I ask.

"So we come to the topic of the end-game, the real end-game. She was afflicted by cancer of the tongue, and it is ironic that the very instrument of speech was afflicted. I was horrified at the news. What would be worse—not to be able to eat or not to be able to speak? But neither occurred. We continued to meet, and then, because of her sensitivity to exposing her disfigurement and, ultimately, physical weakness, we switched to the phone. In our last conversation, she was weak and resigned, 'No more treatments, no more drugs.' She paused. I suppressed an urge to reassure and offer hope, and just listened. Then she simply said, 'Thank you.' And that was it.

"At her funeral, her husband spoke to those assembled. 'She lost her battle with cancer, but won her fight against mental illness.' On a little pedestal next to the lectern from which he spoke rested a small sculpture of a seated woman. After the ceremony, he approached me, sculpture in hand, and gave it to me. 'Here, I want you to have this. Often when she came back from a session with you I'd ask how it went, and she'd answer, 'Oh—we sat on the floor.' That seated woman rests on a table in my office at the foot of my couch—just as a reminder."

I am tempted to ask him about this reminder, but, realising the time, I pose another question. "How have you responded to someone in a crisis? How do you think about what to do to accompany someone through a crisis and beyond it?"

Charles begins by speaking about the problem of diagnosis, and, rather than a diversion, I realise this is his way into the question. "The *DSM* in any form is marginal to my process of thinking about a diagnosis. When you are with someone who is in schizophrenia, you don't need a scorecard to know that! He's incomprehensible, out of touch, and he evokes something uncanny in you. You just work to establish some kind of communication.

"Once, I worked with a young man whose discourse was absolutely haywire. Oh, you could follow one or two sentences, but to string them together—it was like engaging a barbed wire entanglement. We received him in the day hospital from a state hospital where he had been transferred from a local hospital. He had been admitted there four months before, after he drove into a toll-booth on an expressway. He was intoxicated with alcohol and when he was taken to the local hospital it was obvious that he was also floridly psychotic. And so we received him at the day hospital. He was reclusive and said little, and then he developed the thought that one of the female staff was in love with him, became paranoid, and left the programme. I continued to see him, ostensibly to manage his medications. After a few months, he arrived accompanied by his parents. They said that things were not going well at home. He had isolated himself in his room, and they were worried that he was becoming ill again. He sat silently as they spoke. I was up against it. Day hospital was out, and the only alternative seemed to be the hospital, but how to proceed? So, after a bit I described to him what I had heard and said, 'I wonder if you might be interested in meeting more regularly to talk about your situation?' To my utter surprise, he replied, 'Sure—I wouldn't mind going on a roller-coaster ride with someone else's father.' The form of his response is intriguing—the reference to father—but a treatment opened up that lasted for twelve years. He never missed a session; I could set my watch by the time of his arrival for each session.

"There was one difficult enactment, when he appeared again with his parents, having confronted a neighbour with an axe, which he then slammed into the ground between them. After some discussion, it seemed he had wanted 'to set up a boundary'. We continued with weekly sessions. And I learnt that he began to attend art workshops at the mental health centre, eventually having an exhibition there. I asked him if he'd care to bring in some of his art work. 'No,' he intoned. So much for curiosity!

"Again, he surprised me one day when he described in detail a 'primal scene' encounter with his father. 'This has been bothering me my whole life.' By this time he had wanted to come in every other week, and, given this session, I asked if he'd care to come in weekly to work on this. 'No,' he again intoned.

"Some time later, after I returned from my vacation to resume our sessions, I took note of how dishevelled—schizophrenic—he appeared. I recalled Searles' comment about how one of his patients appeared to be a monument to his incompetence as an analyst. Then it occurred to me: not only had I been on vacation, but he had been on one of his own as well, his parents having left him at home alone as they went off to Florida for several weeks. He managed this time alone quite well."

I ask Charles, "Do you think he has created a kind of compensatory organisation?"

"Yeah, probably he has. He's identified as an artist at the mental health centre, and he's getting on in life, and that's good enough."

I return to my questions. "I want to ask you about transference. What aspects of transference come to the fore with someone who is psychotic? Is it different than with someone who is neurotic?"

"The diagnosis is not always clear," Charles muses. "I'm thinking of a case I presented recently that might fit Miller's idea of 'ordinary psychosis'. This refers to someone who, for the most part, functions fairly well, but might have had a crisis from which they emerge either unscathed or with minimal residual symptoms. It is as if they have been perched on a chair with one leg missing—so long as they do not lean the wrong way, they maintain themselves in balance.

"The case in question is that of a woman I have seen now for six years. She came to me after a brief hospitalisation for an acute suicidal state—fantasying jumping into the Chicago River—but instead telling her boss about it. She would come in regularly for a time and then disappear, only to re-emerge, wanting to meet again for a while. She would ask for advice, and I did not respond. One day, her primary care physician wanted to change the medication I had been prescribing because 'no psychiatrist prescribes doses this low'. She was frightened, telling me how the medication was just right for her. A bit later, when another bid for advice went unanswered, she exclaimed, 'Oh, you really want to know what I'm thinking!' She said this rather excitedly and then produced a dream in which she was swept up by a force that lifted her out of a confined space where she could see herself dimly reflected on its marble walls. Over the past few months she has taken responsibility for her sessions, calling if she will be late or can't come in because of newfound work. She is pretty rational, certainly not delusional. Is she psychotic? Someone who looks rational *can* be in the psychotic structure. I am thinking of Lacan's metaphor for suppletion, the three-legged stool; it's perfectly functional, until you suddenly need that fourth leg! Her mother was a paranoid schizophrenic, and my patient was held responsible for her mother's condition. My patient's first job was with the Environmental Protection Agency, which may carry some traces of a mission."

I prompt, "In ordinary psychosis, a distressing element triggers a strange response that does not move into disorganisation or delusion. How do you work with that?"

"You ask me about diagnosis. I have had a hard time with the question of diagnosis. I am thinking of another woman with whom I've worked for decades. She had been terribly traumatised—it seemed since infancy—being subject to physical, verbal, and then sexual abuse at the hands of her father. When we first began, she reported having been considered schizophrenic and then to suffer from a borderline personality disorder. In the beginning she howled because she was terrified to speak. She was never floridly psychotic, and yet, she could not articulate much of her experience. From the start, she wanted to speak, and she had to avoid what she was saying. Her speech was not so much disorganised as elusive. You just never knew what the references were."

I nod, recognising this pattern of speaking. I ask him, "Leaving aside the thorny question of ordinary psychosis, did you modify a psychoanalytic frame to work with her?"

"She saw that I *wanted* to find some way to work with her. She was terribly traumatised and had massive dissociation. Her solution to her fear of speaking was a double session. She could work her way past her fear of speaking, and also come out of the session and manage herself. For my part, I was just holding a frame, and she usually looked like a terrified animal."

"Holding what frame?" I interject.

"My mantra, with permutations, was 'the way out is through this; the only way through is to speak of it'. And she did. But, you know, it's puzzling; she never told a trauma narrative. She just got better, a lot better. It was as though there was some superordinate organisation that got consolidated." He finishes with a rise in his voice, in wonderment. He adds, "The patient thought that the treatment suited her, and since so many treatments failed her, she asked to write about it with me. And we have done that."

The time for our interview ran over, and immediately after it, I thought, "Oh no, Charles has done it again; he's spoken all around the questions, and none of this is going to make sense!" But, I was wrong. While I have edited out *some* of the tangents, what emerged on my first listening to the recording on my iPhone was a remarkably down-to-earth, real and moving conversation. I heard him walk around his speaking, as he wondered, mused, remembered, and laughed at himself. He never positioned himself as the "expert" or even as one who could teach me anything. And, I thought, this is the same man who meets his patients, apparently "doing nothing" while actually doing something utterly necessary.

* * *

The question we are considering is not whether analysis makes sense or not, whether what it puts forth is right or grossly mistaken. I am setting our theories before you because it is the best way to explain the thinking behind analysis, what conditions its approach to the individual patient, and what steps it takes with him. (Freud, 1905e, p. 109)

In the spirit of Freud, I want to reconsider psychoanalysis (modified for psychosis), and in doing so to unravel my position and my thinking about treatment. As I was writing this book, I came to a point of wondering whether or not to go on writing it, in the face of many questions about treating psychosis. This was around the same time that I was considering giving away a Monopoly game that I have had since adolescence, since I do not play it. But, I thought, "Oh, the little Scottie, the thimble, the iron! And all that paper money, useless outside the game; the little cards that instruct you as you go around and around, collecting $200 each time, losing houses, railways, money; the years playing it." I decided to keep the game as a souvenir. I also had a dream in which the windows came in towards my bed, and, at close range, some animal I could not identify appeared with its shoulders covered with snow, a hungry animal. After working with this dream, I decided to stay with writing this book, looking at my own position in relation to my hunger to say something about both psychoanalysis and psychosis. The dream was over-determined and I unravelled many other possibilities, but that matters little here. I am a witness to the experience of psychosis, and I have built a life that includes clinical work in psychoanalysis.

I have worked with psychosis in only two ways, however: in collaboration with colleagues in a treatment situation, and when someone in a crisis has sought me out. In the first instance, I consulted rather than guiding the treatment, and in the second, I accompanied individuals through a terrifying experience for a relatively short time. At the end of this book, I wonder about my position as a clinician in relation to my history, my analysis, and what I may have to offer now.

It is clear to me that you never get "over" psychosis, and I cannot "treat" that which has formed me. No one is cured of psychosis, no more of neurosis. And, at the end of analysis, there remains a remainder (which is also a reminder): this is what caused me, this "untreatable Real" (Apollon, 2006, p. 23). I think of my own position as a fulcrum, the point against which you place a lever to turn what it supports. I am outside psychosis, but I know it intimately and unforgettably. I have been immersed in psychoanalysis as a form of enquiry for most of my life. I have many questions; my enquiry seems to generate more questions than answers. On behalf of my fellow psychotics, I can only offer my thoughts about treatment from the position of a fulcrum, by levering my experience of both psychoanalysis and psychosis.

What does psychoanalysis uniquely have to offer the subject of psychosis? In some very real sense, no more or less that it offers the subject of neurosis: a change in one's construction of the Other, and a resultant change in one's mode of *jouissance*. In neurosis, the analysand is inscribed in the desire of the Other (an Imaginary Other one dances around, second-guessing wishes/whims/ideals), while abjuring any responsibility for the unconscious fantasy that forms *one's own symptom* and has shaped a life narrative and experience. For the neurotic to be free enough to follow her desire, she must become aware of the Other as a construction based on fantasy, decipher her symptom, and find a new mode of *jouissance* grounded in lack and in an ethical position. The idea of *jouissance* in Lacan with respect to neurosis is complex. A working definition (Patsalides & Ror Malone, 2000) might clarify:

> Jouissance is precisely what does not fit into the coherent network of signifiers that are available to the patient—it reflects the difficulty between subject and body, a difficulty that creates a certain excess and indicates that either term is irreducible to the other. (p. 124)

The experience of *jouissance*, originally painful (with hidden sources of pleasure for the neurotic), becomes a remnant of the Real, and an ethical guide to acts that are both unpredictable and incalculable in their effects.

In psychosis, however, the Other is enigmatic, often cruel or perverse, and externalised. The experience of *jouissance* moves through the body quite unpredictably; it is invasive, disorganising, and unbearable. The Other of the psychotic is not open to doubt, or usually decipherable. What then? How to proceed?

I am going first to speak to two groups who do not need or do not seek out (do not want) an analysis. First, there are individuals who, outside of any analytic experience, find a solution to psychosis through a sinthome. They know how to use their unique experience of the Other and *jouissance* to create something utterly original (as Joyce has done) that is not a delusion and also has a value for humanity. The sinthome makes a new social link. All over the world and across decades, for instance, Joyceans explore and celebrate the Other of language Joyce invented and the particular *jouissance* of his language. There might be many more instances of this kind of sinthome-making in human history than we realise. These individuals do not need an analysis.

A second group comprises individuals who have found a solution to the profound disorganisation and enigma of psychosis *in delusion*, and they *do not want to exit what they have constructed* as a working explanation over many years. I think of the artists in Chapters Three and Four. They not only made stunning images guided by singular ideas about themselves, the world, and the cosmos, they also made images beyond social trends or artistic conventions, telling us something vital about our own humanity. They rendered visible what can never be explained or controlled or known fully. I think they are, quite simply, the truest artists among us. They do not need analysis.

Who, then, might come to an analyst, seeking a way through psychosis? And who might seek out a Lacanian analyst in particular? This is increasingly an option in many places in the world. Yet, even if he finds Lacanian analyst, the individual seeking treatment might or might not find a way *through* psychosis. I am thinking of the position of the analyst as a wary companion, one who guides the psychotic around holes in the Symbolic in relation to questions of her existence in order to avert a crisis. The analyst may look for, and help the psychotic to build a suppletion, something that can function to fill in the gaping hole around the missing metaphor of the Name-of-the-Father. In this case, the individual remains vulnerable to the holes in the Symbolic that have never been deciphered or reconstructed. As we saw with Barbara O'Brien in Chapter Six, the only option might be to avoid the situation(s) that can trigger madness. Perhaps for some people this is a good solution, but I am not satisfied with this solution; it does not go far enough. The idea of the missing metaphor of the Name-of-the-Father and/or the fear of a crisis on the analyst's side acts as a barrier, in my view, to offering a true analytic experience. It also ignores Lacan's late thinking about psychosis and the clinic.

What psychoanalysis offers is a unique experience: a way to construct the impossible-to-know, an invitation to name what cannot even be recalled, a place to speak (freely) as a risk one takes again and again, without knowing the consequence—until the arc of a new order emerges over years—that effects the Real body of *jouissance* and opens a new ethics. The very idea of undertaking such work with a psychotic might seem daft, or worse, possibly harmful. But I know this work is possible from my own experience. And I know it is possible as it resounds with accounts of analysis by those analysts who find a way *through psychosis* with their patients, including the GIRFIC analysts in Quebec, Canada, and my two colleagues in this chapter.

The question is—why is the option of psychoanalysis so seldom considered? This question is bound up not only in how we consider psychosis—what it is, how it works—but also with the problem of who, indeed, has access to psychoanalysis. Psychoanalytic treatment seems to be a castle surrounded by the great moat of class privilege (paying for an analysis is simply not possible for many), and a lack of imagination on the part of those who might actually offer such treatment, particularly for psychosis. Yet, in his day, Freud and others envisioned free psychoanalytic clinics (Danto, 2005). Although most institutes and Lacanian Schools offer discounts in their clinics, we have yet to take Freud up on this radical possibility.

What does it mean to be on the edge of psychosis, on the threshold yet not mad? Of course, this is the position of those who do not experience a crisis because they have found another solution. Is the psychotic, as a structure, always at the verge of psychosis? In the absence of an analysis that is a real analysis, that breaks into questions of existence (and also risks a crisis), I think it is the case that the psychotic is always on the verge of madness. However he or she keeps madness at bay, this is a real vulnerability. For this reason, many analysts continue to see psychotic patients over decades, a treatment that has no terminal point, as a provisional solution.

However, I think there is a threshold experience of a different sort, which comes following a long and real analysis. What is vital in analysis is that the psychotic name the delusion (along with its origin), and experience the fall of the Other as a perverse, omniscient Other. With that shattering comes the realisation that one has no *appointed* place or purpose, but must make a place for oneself. Then, language will not carry all of meaning (magically and externally imposed everywhere). A measure of *jouissance* is lost; a delusion (or a suppletion) is in ruins, and one takes a newly responsible place in a social link. And what remains? What remains is what is there: a remnant of *jouissance*—the Real of the body and the unconscious as unknown. The psychotic then stands at a different threshold, at the edge of the void of her existence, close to the Real on one side and, on the other side, she makes a commitment to the world with its imperfections.

What, in analysis, makes it possible to move through psychosis, not to a place beyond it, but to a new threshold? If the problematic at the start is that signs, codes, omens, voices, private epiphanies inscribe meanings that cannot be questioned, this experience must yield to questions. Perhaps, at first, they are the questions of the analyst, but, crucially, they become the questions of the psychotic. Analysis is, then, a work of construction. It is the analysand who creates links between her particular madness and lived experience. He discovers names for things he has never been able to speak. The puzzles of her existence are simply that: puzzles that she works out in relation to life and death, social existence, and the meaning of her life—puzzles that are never entirely solved, but lived. This work could involve invoking new metaphors and building on them to link the known events of one's life with unknown truths in the chain of human history, as all of us must do. One does not exit the structure of psychosis: it has formed the very ground for the analysis and remains.

This work involves at least some deciphering. It is what psychoanalysis offers. While the psychotic experiences holes in the Symbolic and the Real takes precedence, shaping language and the body, this position does not mean that *nothing* can be deciphered. To decipher is to read, to read what is difficult to understand, and to interpret, to link what is obscure to something else that can represent it in a new light. If the analyst takes, as Barri Belnap said, "a side by side position", it is possible to wonder with a patient about all sorts of things requiring a reading or a radical re-reading. But the psychotic is allergic to false authority, to expertise imposed, to any stance that obscures what is both real in his experience and true. The place of the analyst, as it is for Charles Turk, is sometimes to "do nothing" when the "nothing" of the analyst is an active waiting for the psychotic to risk her soul with her speech.

While I have formulated my thinking along the lines of a Lacanian analysis here (this is what saturates my experience of the clinic now), my own first analysis was with a Freudian object-relations analyst. The theory did not matter; whatever theory he had learnt he *put to work in his way* with psychotics, and that made it possible for me *to find my way* beyond a crisis and into a new life trajectory, otherwise unthinkable. He listened carefully to my speech, even when I was disorganised, welcomed my paintings and writings, even when "I" did not create them, to make a space for what has been impossible for me to convey to anyone. But it was a Lacanian approach that led me to see that the Other (of my translations) was not what I had thought, and I could never return to that position because it all came from *within me*—every bit of delusion that seemed given from without came from within, crossing generations to transmit to me. And then scraps of musical words, nonsense-words, came back to me, outside psychosis and beyond any meaning, as joyful. There is no going back from that.

The effective analyst for the psychotic, in my view, is in the position of what Lacan called the *Father of the Name* (Lacan, Seminar XXIII). The analyst makes a place for the psychotic to name what was once both overwhelmingly enigmatic and also known—not as knowledge, but as something that registered on the body. This *Father of the Name* is not in the desire or discourse of the Other. Rather, his position is a matter of naming, saying the Real, where saying is an act (Soler, 2014). This saying, in fact, propels the work of deciphering *what can be deciphered* (which is not everything). For Lacan, the Symbolic makes a hole, an irreducible hole (or lack) and signifiers circle around it—these are the signifiers of the desire of the Other. However, names are not signifiers in this sense. "Names come from the true hole of the unconscious, the Real, the void." This hole, Lacan says, "spits out the Names-of-the-Father" (Soler, 2014, p. 156).

If we recognise that the analyst's position as the *Father of the Name* safeguards a space for saying the Real, this position has an effect on the analysand. It makes it possible for her to speak from the Real, bringing elements of delusion, moments outside of time–space–reality into a naming the analyst supports and enquires about, so that the psychotic risks what she thinks she knows, and enters the unknown. Importantly, the analyst cannot be in the position of the *Father of the Name* and skirt the psychotic's questions of existence in order to avert a crisis. That, in my view, is a matter of ethics. It is why I think that accompanying someone through psychosis requires collaboration and consultation among trusted colleagues working together. This approach creates a safety net and a way through a crisis. The *Father of the Name* makes a space for the unconscious to speak, where speaking always entails a risk. And the effect of the *Father of the Name* is that the Names-of-the-Father start coming from the analysand, to knit her speaking to the Real in a social link. It becomes possible, in this way, to name what one has never been able to say or know, and also come, at the end, to what one must live with as a remnant of madness, a kernel of *jouissance*. Even the neurotic must come to this place, and it is harder and may take longer for her to do so.

The analyst, in my view, is not one who *treats* psychosis. Psychosis is *beyond treatment*, unless one reduces it to a disease or a problematic to be fixed. It is neither of those for me, and I cannot treat what has formed me. No more can anyone. What that made us lies beyond us. It came before speaking, and remains up to our deaths, and analysis does not alter that. I shall underline this point through an excerpt from a lecture Lacan gave in Geneva in 1975, in which he spoke about his own children:

> I have observed a number of small children closely, even if they were only my own. The fact that a child says, *perhaps, not yet,* before he is able to construct a sentence properly, proves that there is something in him through which everything is sieved, whereby the water of language happens to leave something behind as it passes, some detritus which he will play with, indeed which he will be forced to cope with. This is what all this non-reflected activity leaves him with— debris—to which, later on, because he is premature, there will be added problems that will frighten him . . . (Lacan, 1989, p. 10)

This is one of the clearest and most eloquent observations of Lacan. Of his children, he says, "the water of language happens to leave something behind as it passes, some detritus which he will play with . . ." These are bits of language linked with the Real, with the body enjoying, and the body afraid. How we each play with this problematic, cope with it, forms *what we become*.

Psychosis is a coat I still carry; and though its shape has been altered almost beyond recognition through my own analysis, it is still my coat. It becomes me. I fling it over my shoulder and it flaps like a large bird, or a sail of canvas. Wind rips through it, shivers it. You cannot analyse the coat *itself*. Speaking or singing to me, it knots, furls, wheels, and turns back to silence, supported by the roaring void. I carry it, and it floats behind me. It has written this book with me.

This coat is all I have to offer my fellow psychotics, if I am invited to accompany them—whether as a friend, or an ally, or as an analyst.

REFERENCES

Apollon, W. (2006). The untreatable real. *Umbr(a): A Journal of the Unconscious*: 23–40.

Apollon, W., Bergeron, D., & Cantin, L. (2002). *After Lacan: Clinical Practice and the Subject of the Unconscious*. Albany, NY: State University of New York.

Artaud, A. (1958). *The Theatre and Its Double*, M. C. Richards (Trans.). New York: Grove Weidenfeld.

Artaud, A. (1976). *Antonin Artaud: Selected Writings*, S. Sontag (Ed). New York: Farrar, Straus & Giroux.

Artaud, A. (1978). Centre-noeuds. In: *Suppôts et suppliciations* (p. 26). Paris: Gallimard.

Artaud, A. (2008). *50 Drawings to Murder Magic*, D. Nicholson-Smith (Trans.). London: Seagull Books.

Ashbery, J. (1999). *Girls on the Run*. New York: Farrar, Straus and Giroux.

Ayral-Clause, O. (2002). *Camille Claudel: A Life*. New York: Harry N. Abrams.

Bataille, G. (1988 [1949]). The cruel practice of art. In: *Oeuvres Completes, Vol. XI*. Paris: Gallimard. Translation through Supervert32, supervert.com.

Beckett, S. (1994)[1951]. *The Trilogy: Molloy, Malone Dies, The Unnamable*. London: Calder.

Berger, J. (2011). *Bento's Sketchbook*. New York: Pantheon.

Bervin, J., & Werner, M. (Eds.) (2013). *The Gorgeous Nothings: Emily Dickinson's Envelope Poems*. New York: New Directions.

Blanchot, M. (1995)[1980]. *Writing of the Disaster*, A. Smock (Trans.). Lincoln, NE: University of Nebraska Press.

Brisley, S. (2014). Note to Thomas Röske on About Barbara Suckfull. Accessed at: http:/stuartbrisley.com.

Campion, J. (1990). *An Angel at My Table*. Film.

Cantin, L. (2009). An effective treatment of psychosis with psychoanalysis in Quebec City, since 1982. *Annual Review of Critical Psychology, 7*: 286–319.

Clausen, B. C., Jadi, I., & Douglas, C. (1996). *Beyond Reason Art and Psychosis: Works from the Prinzhorn Collection*. Berkeley, CA: University of California Press.

Cody, J. (1971). *After Great Pain: The Inner Life of Emily Dickinson*. Cambridge, MA: Belkap Press of Harvard University Press.

Covington, M., He, C., Brown, C., Naci, L., McClain, J., Sirmon-Fjordbak, B., Semple, J., & Brown, J. (2005). Schizophrenia and the structure of language. *Schizophrenia Research, 77*: 85–98.

Danto, E. A. (2005). *Freud's Free Clinics: Psychoanalysis and Social Justice, 1918–1938*. New York: Columbia University Press.

Davoine, F., & Gaudillierre, M. (2004). *History Beyond Trauma*, S. Fairfield (Trans.). New York: Other Press.

Declercq, F. (2004). Lacan's concept of the real of jouissance: clinical illustrations and implications. *Psychoanalysis, Culture and Society, 9*: 237–251.

Deleuze, G. (1993)[1969]. *The Logic of Sense*, C. Boudas (Ed.), M. Lestor & C. Stivale (Trans.), New York: Columbia University Press.

Deleuze, G., & Guattari, F. (2004)[1972]. *Anti-Oedipus*, R. Hurley, M. Seem, & H. R. Lane (Trans.). London: Continuum.

Eliot, T. S. (1940). *East Coker*. London: Faber.

Ellman, R. (1983)[1959]. *James Joyce*. Oxford and New York: Oxford University Press.

Eluard, P. (1981). "ARP", Eat it Alive, A. Levin. *University of Colorado at Boulder Creative Writing Program, 3*(5) (December, 1981).

Ferrier, J. L. (1998). *Outsider Art*. Paris: Finest Sa/Pierre Terrail Editions.

Fink, B. (2007). *Fundamentals of Psychoanalytic Technique: A Lacanian Approach for Practitioners*. New York: W. W. Norton.

Frame, J. (1951). *The Lagoon and Other Stories*. Christchurch: Caxton.

Frame, J. (1962). *The Edge of the Alphabet*. New York: George Braziller.

Frame, J. (1982a)[1960]. *Owls Do Cry*. New York: George Braziller.

Frame, J. (1982b). *To the Is-land* [Volume one of autobiography. New York: George Braziller.

Frame, J. (1984a). *An Angel at My Table* [Volume two of autobiography]. New York: George Braziller.

Frame, J. (1984b). *The Envoy from Mirror City* [Volume three of autobiography]. Auckland: Century Hutchinson.

Frame, J. (2007). *Towards Another Summer*. Auckland: Vintage.

Franklin, F. W. (Ed.) (1981). *The Manuscripts Books of Emily Dickinson: A Facsimile Edition*. Cambridge, MA: Belkap Press of Harvard University Press.

Freud, S. (1904a). Freud's psycho-analytic procedure. *S. E.*, 7: 249–256. London: Hogarth Press.

Freud, S. (1905e). *Fragment of an Analysis of a Case of Hysteria. S. E.*, 7: 7–122. London: Hogarth.

Freud, S. (2002[1927]). The question of lay analysis. In: A. Phillips (Ed.), A. Bance (Trans.), *Wild Analysis* (pp. 93–160). London: Penguin.

Galchen, R. (2010). From the pencil zone: Robert Walser's masterworklets. *Harpers*, May: 73–78.

Gilman, C. (2013). *Dickinson/Walser Pencil Sketches*. New York: The Drawing Center.

Harrow, M., & Jobe, T. (2013). Does long-term treatment of schizophrenia with antipsychotic medications facilitate recovery? *Schizophrenia Bulletin, 39* (5): 962–965.

Heller-Roazen, D. (2007). Phantoms. *Cabinet Magazine, 25*. Available at https://secure.cabinetmagazine.org/store/category/13.

Ingold, T. (2007). Language, music and notation. In: *Lines: A Brief History* (pp. 6–38). London: Routledge.

Jacobson, M., & Gaze, T. (2013). *An Anthology of Asemic Handwriting*. Flanders: Uitgeverij.

Jaynes, J. (1990)[1976]. *The Origins of Consciousness in the Breakdown of the Bicameral Mind*. New York: Houghton Mifflin.

Johnson, T. H. (Ed.) (1961). *Complete Poems of Emily Dickinson*. Boston, MA: Little, Brown.

Joyce, J. (1999)[1939]. *Finnegans Wake*. New York: Penguin.

Joyce, J. (2000)[1914]. *Dubliners*. London: Penguin.

Joyce, J. (2000)[1916]. *Portrait of the Artist as a Young Man*. London: CRW.

Joyce, J. (2003). *The "Finnegans Wake" Notebooks at Buffalo. Notebook VI.B.I*, V. Deane, D. Ferrer, T. Joyce, & G. Lernout (Eds.). Turnhout, Belgium: Brepols.

Joyce, J. (2010)[1922]. *Ulysses*. London: Wordsworth Editions.

Kentridge, W. (2014). *Six Drawing Lessons*. Cambridge, MA: Harvard University Press.

King, M. (2001). *Wrestling with the Angel: A Life of Janet Frame*. London: Picador/Macmillan.

King, M. (2004). Janet Frame. *Guardian*, 30 January. Accessed at: http:/ theguardian.com.

Lacan, J. (1974–1975). *Real, Symbolic, Imaginary: The Seminar of Jacques Lacan, Book XXII*, C. Gallagher (Trans.). Accessed at: http:/lacanin ireland.com.

Lacan, J. (1975–1976). *Joyce and the Sinthome: The Seminar of Jacques Lacan, Book XXIII*. C. Gallagher (Trans.) from unedited French manuscripts. Personal copy provided by Gallagher.

Lacan, J. (1981)[1977]. Preface to the English Language Edition. In: *Four Fundamental Concepts of Psychoanalysis, The Seminar of Jacques Lacan, Book XI* (pp. vii–x). New York: W. W. Norton.

Lacan, J. (1989). Geneva lecture on the symptom. *Analysis*, 1: 7–26.

Lacan, J. (1997)[1981]. *The Psychoses, The Seminar of Jacques Lacan, Book III* (1955–1956), J.-A. Miller (Ed.), R. Grigg (Trans.). New York: W. W. Norton.

Lacan, J. (2006a). *Ecrits: The First Complete Edition in English*, B. Fink (Trans.). New York: W. W. Norton.

Lacan, J. (2006b). On a question prior to any possible treatment of psychosis. In: *Écrits: The First Complete Edition in English*, B. Fink (Trans.) (pp. 445–488). New York: W. W. Norton.

Laurent, E. (2012). Psychosis, or radical belief in the symptom, A. Price (Trans.). Accessed at: http:/lacan.com.

Lawson, J. S., McGhie, A., & Chapman, J. (1964). Perception of speech in schizophrenia. *British Journal of Psychiatry*, 110: 375–380.

MacGregor, J. (1990). *Dwight Macintosh: The Boy Who Time Forgot*. Oakland, CA: Creative Growth Center.

MacGregor, J. (2002). *Henry Darger: In the Realms of the Unreal*. New York: Delana Greenidge Editions.

Maslen, M., & Southern, J. (2011). *Drawing Projects: An Exploration of the Language of Drawing*. London: Black Dog.

Maugham, W. S. (1992)[1938]. *The Summing Up*. New York: Penguin Classics.

McCreedy, J. (2010). Everyword for oneself but Code for us all! The shapes of sigla in Finnegans Wake. *Genetic Joyce Studies*, 10. Accessed at: http:/ antwerpjamesjoycecenter.com.

McElheny, J. (2013). Visual forms for words: overlaps of art and literature in Emily Dickinson and Robert Walser. In: *Dickinson/Walser Pencil Sketches* (pp. 51–72). New York: The Drawing Center.

McLean, R. (2003). *Recovered, Not Cured: A Journey Through Schizophrenia*. Crows Nest, Australia: Allen & Unwin.

Miller, J. A. (2009). Ordinary psychosis revisited. *Psychoanalytic Notebooks of the European School of Psychoanalysis, 19:* 139–168.

Moncrieff, J. (2013). *The Bitterest Pills: The Troubling Story of Antipsychotic Drugs*. London: Palgrave Macmillan.

Morganthaler, W. (1992)[1921]. *Art and Madness: The Life and Works of Adolph Wölfli*. Lincoln, NE: University of Nebraska Press.

Muller, J. (2014). Sublimation and das ding in Mahler's Symphony No. 8. In: *A Spirit that Impels: Play, Creativity and Psychoanalysis* (pp. 53–74). London: Karnac.

North, C. (2002). *Welcome, Silence: My Triumph over Schizophrenia* (revised edn). Lima, OH: Academic Renewal Press.

O'Brien, B. (2011). *Operators and Things: The Inner Life of a Schizophrenic*. Los Angeles, CA: Silver Birch Press.

Olivier, B. (2009). *Philosophy and Psychoanalytic Theory: Collected Essays*. New York: Peter Lang.

Parnas, J. (2000). The self and intentionality in the pre-psychotic stages of schizophrenia. In: D. Zahavi (Ed.), *Exploring the Self: Philosophical and Psychopathological Perspectives on Self-Experience*. Amsterdam: John Benjamins.

Patsalides, A., & Ror Malone, K. (2000). Jouissance in the cure. In: R. Malone & S. Friedlander (Eds.), *The Subject of Lacan: A Lacanian Reader for Psychologists* (pp. 123–134). Albany, NY: State University of New York Press.

Prinzhorn, H. (1972)[1922]. *The Artistry of the Mentally Ill*, E. von Brockdoff (Trans.). New York: Springer.

Redmond, J. (2014). *Ordinary Psychosis and the Body: A Contemporary Lacanian Approach*. London: Palgrave Macmillan.

Rilke, R.M. (1939). *Duino Elegies*. New York: W.W. Norton

Rivers, C. (2004). *Donald Mitchell: Right Here, Right Now*. Oakland, CA: Creative Growth Art Center.

Robinson, W. (2011). *Demons in the Age of Light: A Memoir of Psychosis and Recovery*. Port Townsend, WA: Process Media.

Rogers, A. (1995). *A Shining Affliction*. New York: Penguin Viking.

Rogers, A. (2006). *The Unsayable*. New York: Random House.

Rogers, A. (2015). "Emily, in her Room," In: M. Medeiros (Ed.), *A Mighty Room: a Collection of Poems Written in Emily Dickinson's Bedroom* (p. 32). Amherst, MA: Emily Dickinson Museum

Rosenbaum, B., & Sonne, H. (1986). *The Language of Psychosis*. New York: New York University Press.

Sachs, O. (2012). *Hallucinations*. New York: Vintage Books.

Saks, E. (2007). *The Center Cannot Hold: My Journey Through Madness*. New York: Hyperion.

Sass, L., & Parnas, J. (2003). Schizophrenia, consciousness and the self. *Schizophrenia Bulletin*, 29(3): 427–444.

Schreber, D. P. (2001)[1903]. *Memoirs of My Nervous Illness*, R. Dinnage (Trans.). New York: New York Review of Books.

Smock, A. (1995). Translator's remarks. In: M Blanchot, *The Writing of the Disaster* (pp. vii–xiii). Lincoln, NE: University of Nebraska Press.

Soler, C. (2014). *Lacan: The Unconscious Reinvented*. London: Karnac.

Steele, K., & Berman, C. (2001). *The Day the Voices Stopped: A Memoir of Madness and Hope*. New York: Basic Books.

Thevoz, M. (1995). *Art Brut*. London: Academy Editions.

Thorne, T. (2012). Heavenly city—John Devlin's utopian visions. [Interview with John Devlin.] *Raw Vision*, 77: 42–45.

Tranströmer. T. (1995). Memories Look at Me. In: *For the Living and the Dead: Poems and a Memoir* (pp. 25–45). New York: HarperCollins.

Tranströmer, T. (2006)[1987]. *The Great Enigma: New Collected Poems*, R. Fulton (Trans.). New York: New Directions.

Tranströmer, T. (2011)[1987]. *New Collected Poems*, R. Fulton (Trans.). Tarset: Bloodaxe Books.

Walser, R. (1999)[1909]. *Jakob von Gunten*. C. Middleton (Trans.). New York: New York Review.

Walser, R. (2000)[1925]. *The Robber*. S. Bernofsky (Trans.). Lincoln, NE: Bison Books.

Walser, R. (2009)[1906]. *The Tanners*. S. Bernofsky (Trans.). New York: New Directions.

Walser, R. (2010). *The Microscripts*. S. Bernofsky (Trans.). New York: New Directions.

Weisskopf-Joelson, E. (1988). *Father, Have I Kept my Promise? Madness as Seen from Within*. West Lafayette, IN: Purdue University Press.

Whitaker, R. (2010). *Anatomy of an Epidemic: Magic Bullets, Psychiatric Drugs, and the Astonishing Rise of Mental Illness in America*. New York: Crown.

Vanheule, S. (2011). *The Subject of Psychosis: A Lacanian Perspective*. New York: Palgrave/Macmillan.

Vanheule, S. (2014). *Diagnosis and the DSM: A Critical Review*. London: Palgrave Pivot.

Yeiser, B. (2014). *Mind Estranged: My Journey from Schizophrenia and Homelessness to Recovery*. Amazon: Create Space, Kindle Edition.

INDEX